OTHER TITLES OF INTEREST FROM ST. LUCIE PRESS

The Executive Guide to Implementing Quality Systems

Peter Mears
Department of Management
University of Louisville
Louisville, Kentucky

Frank Voehl
Strategy Associates, Inc.
Coral Springs, Florida

KOGAN PAGE

First published in 1995 in the USA by
St. Lucie Press ©
Published in 1995 in the UK by Kogan Page Ltd.

Kogan Page Limited
120 Pentonville Road
London N1 9JN

British Library Cataloguing in Publication Data

A CIP record for this book is available from the British Library.

ISBN 0 7494 1703 X

Printed and bound in the USA

Contents

Preface

You are about to begin a journey toward Continuous Quality Improvement (CQI). This may be a difficult journey because you are going to be asked to do a lot of thinking about how to operationalize the CQI philosophy. After reading about a concept, you will be asked to contribute to exercises designed to identify the management systems needed to support quality improvement.

It is your job to make contributions that move the process forward. Be innovative and explore options. Avoid defending what you are currently doing. Instead of thinking "That won't work here," think "What will work here?"

At the risk of repetition, be innovative and explore options. If you feel skeptical about the CQI philosophy, and then proceed to install CQI, do you believe your employees will really embrace the concept of quality improvement? Probably not. Management must take the lead in installing CQI in an organization. Therefore, if you are unsure about a topic, speak up. If you can shed insight into how a problem might be solved, share that insight with others.

This structure is only the first step in your journey toward improved quality. The next step is the big one: installing the concepts for CQI. As a leader, you realize that getting top performance—and becoming a world-class organization—is possible, but it takes a lot more than common sense management to make it happen. It takes a leadership team of people who are dedicated to bringing out the best in people and who reinforce the behaviors necessary to achieve the vision and goals. This workbook is simply about identifying the support systems that generate desirable outcomes and reinforcing them through positive actions.

Credits

Exercises 2, 3, 5 to 9, 13 to 15, 17 to 19, 22 to 24, 26 to 28, and 30 to 35 were provided by Management Consultant Specialists and are found in the workbook "Quality Leadership" (Mears, 1993). Exercises 1, 4, 10 to 12, 16, 20, 21, 25, and 29 were provided by Strategy Associates, Inc. and are found in the workbook "Leadership and Management Quality: A Quality Council Workshop" (Voehl, 1994).

Authors

Peter Mears is President of Management Consultant Specialists and Professor of Management at the College of Business and Public Administration, University of Louisville. Trained as an industrial engineer, he has extensive experience in the private sector with such companies as Goodyear and Martin Marietta.

A former Malcolm Baldrige National Quality Award examiner, Dr. Mears now serves as a consultant to several firms. He is currently involved with installing a quality management program at the University of Louisville, where he has also created courses and curricula for teaching quality on both the undergraduate and graduate levels.

Dr. Mears is a member of the Academy of Management, the Association for Quality and Participation, and the American Society for Quality Control, where he conducts ISO 9000 certification courses.

Frank Voehl has had a twenty-year career in quality management, productivity improvement, and related fields. He has written more than 200 articles, papers, and books on the subject of quality. Mr. Voehl has consulted on quality and productivity issues, as well as measurement system implementation, for hundreds of companies (many Fortune 500 corporations). As general manager of FPL Qualtec, he was influential in the FPL Deming Prize process. He is a member of strategic planning committees with the ASQC and AQP and has assisted the IRS in planning as a member of the Commissioner's Advisory Group (CAG).

An Industrial Engineering graduate from St. John's University in New York City, Mr. Voehl has been a visiting professor and lecturer at N.Y.U. and the University of Miami, where he helped establish the framework for the Quality Institute. He is currently President and CEO of Strategy Associates, Inc. and a visiting professor at Florida International University.

Chapter 1

Leadership for Continuous Quality Improvement

Introduction to Leadership

Leadership is defined as "the capacity or ability to show the way by going in advance; the act of guiding a course, behavior or opinion of others by playing a principal or guiding role, especially in the creation of the excellent department or organization."[1] The terms *leadership* and *excellence* are permanently intertwined. What is the excellent department or organization? Just what does it look like?

In *Managing for Excellence,* the seminal work on leadership by Bradford and Cohen, the excellent department is described as follows:[2]

> It is a department that works close to its potential, instead of with inertia and resistance. Its members share a commitment to making the unit extraordinarily successful in accomplishing agreed-on organizational objectives. The focus is on quality, on genuinely collaborative team effort, on confronting differences about work without petty infighting, and on continual attention to the development of members as integral to achieving the task.
>
> The concern for excellence in such an organization is not the exclusive property of the leader. Instead, all members share this concern and are prepared to do whatever is necessary in order to achieve expectations...In an excellent department, everyone worries about the whole system and

> takes initiative to see that problems are dealt with and objectives met...The concern for task accomplishment includes a strong emphasis on quality—of products, services, and members themselves.
>
> There is a clarity about the department's and organizational goals which provides a clear focus on work. These goals are accepted by all and are used as a basis for making decisions and guiding actions. People are directly told about poor performance and are helped to improve while continued mediocrity leads to the search for a better job. Thus, there is no "deadwood"...In this type of organization, information is freely transmitted among members and the boss. Outstanding performers are encouraged to set even higher goals instead of being pulled down to the safe average. Finally, value is placed on diversity. Different views about how the goal is attained are allowed to surface and various approaches are encouraged, while conformity in thought and style is discouraged.

All this may sound a bit utopian. Although the portrait of Bradford and Cohen's *excellent department* is an idealized state, these conditions can be witnessed to some degree in occasional pockets of leadership, led by senior managers who do things in special ways. But what causes the discrepancy between actual and potential performance? The problem, according to Bradford and Cohen and verified by the authors' own experience, lies with the model of leadership used by most managers—a model appropriate to a previous era but now outdated and outmoded for eliciting maximum performance in complex, contemporary organizations.[2] This model is based on the old command-and-control style, in which all power and authority flow through the manager, who solves all the problems and calls all the shots in the "Lone Ranger" style of managing.[3] In pointing out the problem with conventional management, we are not advocating that all the leadership development of the past decade be thrown out.

Excellence demands budget and control systems and formalized ways to reward, prompt, and appraise, as well as long-range planning and forecasting systems. The dilemma for the leader is not whether control needs to be exercised, but rather how to exercise control without weakening the motivation of those with energy, empowerment, and enthusiasm. A new form of leadership is needed to move beyond mere participative management and into the realm of leadership for continuous quality improvement.

Let's examine the role of leadership more closely to see what cultural change is needed at each stage of development. Kouzes and Posner[4] have developed some original research to study the cultural behavior of leaders who achieve exceptional results. Their studies of these high achievers reveal a pattern indicating that 80% of the time they are engaged in activities that fall into the following seven categories of behavior:

- **Challenge the process**—Leaders are pioneers who seek new opportunities and are willing to change the status quo. They realize that failure to change and adapt leads to mediocrity, and, therefore, they innovate and experiment in order to improve the organization.

- **Inspire a shared vision**—Leaders look to the future and beyond the horizon, with dreams of what can and might be. They believe that if people work together, they can achieve the excellent organization that others just dream about. They are expressive and attract followers through genuine and skillful communication. They are truthful and do not deceive. They show others how common interests can be met through commitment to shared goals.

- **Enable others to act and succeed**—Leaders realize that they are rewarded for enabling others to achieve results. They realize that they can't do it alone and, therefore, infuse people with enthusiasm and commitment. They are persuasive people who develop relationships based on mutual trust and working toward collaborative goals. They stress participation in decision making and problem solving, and they actively involve others in planning, allowing them to make decisions even if it means making mistakes. Reasonable risk taking is encouraged and much discretion is allowed. Finally, leaders empower others to become leaders in their own way instead of just doing as they are told. This requires an ability to manage ambiguity and take responsibility for others.

- **Model their values and beliefs**—Leaders are clear about their values and beliefs and have standards which are clear to all.

They stand up for what they believe in, and they communicate this to all their people. They keep things on course by behaving consistently with these values and modeling how they expect others to act. In other words, they "walk their talk."

- **Persuade to new heights**—Leaders persuade us that the impossible is within reach and the unimaginable is just around the corner. They split projects into small achievable steps to create opportunities for small wins. They make it easier for others to achieve goals by focusing on these steps and identifying key priorities, often by setting examples and behaving in ways that are consistent with their values and beliefs.

- **Encourage and support**—Leaders encourage people to achieve difficult goals and targets. They persist in their efforts by relating recognition to accomplishments and giving frequent feedback. They let others know that their efforts are appreciated and go out of their way to say thank you for a job well done. They communicate the successes and celebrate the wins. Finally, leaders nurture a team philosophy and a sustained effort by encouraging others to put even more into what they do.

- **Focus on the customer**—Leaders have learned how to make the customer feel like a "king" and keep customers satisfied for life.

Monday Morning Mirror Issues

Wait a minute. TQM isn't mystical --

Unless I put common sense in that category.

Exercise 1

Leadership Profile

Instructions:

Your CEO has asked your team to investigate the role of the leader in implementing continuous quality improvement. This could be the first step in the implementation of continuous quality improvement, and your CEO wants to be sure that the leader's role is well understood. Using the information you have and Worksheet 1, develop a profile of the leader of the future.

Take about 20 minutes to complete this assignment. Assign a spokesperson to report your team's results.

Worksheet 1

Profile of a Leader

The following attributes are found in the leader of the future:

Continuous Quality Improvement

Various names and acronyms have been used to identify the concept of Continuous Quality Improvement (CQI). Originally, it was called Total Quality Management (TQM), but there is a problem with that name. Quality is **not** a management program. Quality improvement requires that **all** people at all levels of the organization work together closely to improve the quality of goods or services. If quality improvement is viewed simply as a management problem or, worse yet, a management program, employees may be reluctant to fully commit themselves to the effort that will be required to improve quality.

Second, and equally important, TQM sounds like a typical management program. Such programs tend to come and go, however. That is, employee reaction to a new management program will likely consist of "burying their heads in the sand" until the fad passes. However, the very survival of an organization depends on the quality of its goods and services. Quality improvement cannot be viewed as a fad. In fact, an effective quality improvement system will require a change in the culture of the organization. You cannot simply send everyone to a training program and magically transform your organization into a quality organization. An infrastructure is needed to promote and sustain a CQI system.

Finally, where do the new TQM converts and preachers who have joined the quality field in the past four or five years fit into the picture, especially those whose background in the field is purely academic or consists at its core of nothing more than attending numerous seminars or reading the latest popular quality books? What they have succeeded in doing is jamming so much into the TQM tool kit that many organizations are being overwhelmed as the bag bursts in their hands. And what about all the good quality assurance and quality control programs? Have they become obsolete as well?

For these and other reasons, the term CQI will be used throughout this senior management leadership workbook to identify quality systems. While we are not at all against using a great deal of what the TQM concept tries to introduce, we do not think it should all try to fit under one umbrella. According to Gooden and English, a company's quality improvement effort includes at least three distinct categories or attributes: the leadership style employed, the quality systems in place, and the human resource involvement and training programs.[5] Each element must be developed and evaluated separately. TQM tries to put all of these elements under one roof, plus it adds other elements such as strategic planning, empowerment, teams, etc. The result is that this new concoction tends to overwhelm an organization with meetings and activities.

Why isn't this quality improvement system called Just-in-Time, quick response time, SMED (Single Minute Exchange of Dies), TQM, or simply total quality? The answer is simple. The term CQI is used to indicate that we are not discussing a "one-shot" quality improvement effort. We are talking about a system that encourages everyone to become involved in bringing about the continuous improvement of quality as a way of life—a journey rather than a destination.

Continuous Quality Improvement

IS	IS NOT
■ A cultural change	■ An overnight cure
■ Responsibility of top management	■ Delegated to subordinates
■ A systematic way to improve services	■ A new program
■ A structured approach to solving problems	■ "Fighting fires"
■ Conveyed by action	■ Conveyed by slogan
■ Practiced by everyone	■ A specialist discipline
■ Team involved	■ A "Lone Ranger" activity

Several actions must occur in order for senior management and organizations to become seriously committed to improving the quality of their goods, services, and operations. The first and most important of these actions is that senior management must be fully committed to the improvement process. All too often, employees hear about management's commitment to this program or to that program. A demonstrated commitment by management is what leads the continuous quality improvement process.

This is a long-term process, and it requires constant reinforcement by all levels of management. Although we will be discussing various systems to reinforce and sustain a CQI system, these concepts will be of little use unless quality improvement through leadership becomes the top priority of all senior managers.

Quality Improvement Essentials

- **Management commitment leads the quality process**
- **Quality is consistent conformance to customer expectations**
- **Measurement of quality is through indicators of customer satisfaction**
- **The objective is conformance to expectations 100% of the time**
- **Quality is attained by specific improvement projects**

As previously mentioned, managers have traditionally increased their power through controls. Many a manager's job is a "signature cycle" or a "must obtain approval from" type of position. Such processes must not be allowed to continue. However, an organization does not adopt CQI simply because the president issues an administrative memo to that effect. Adopting a CQI philosophy requires a change in the leadership model and in the basic way business is conducted.

Changes Required for CQI		
Issues	**Change from:**	**Change to:**
Defects	Inevitable	Zero defects
Training	Cost	Investment
	Resisted	Way of life
Change		
Time horizon	Short term	Long term
Customers	Take it or leave it	Satisfaction
Vendors	Price	Price and quality
Performance	Cost and schedule	Customer requirements
Information flow	Vertical	Horizontal and vertical
Performance goals	Standards	Better than yesterday
Management role	Enforcer	Coach

The CEO's Role in Continuous Quality Improvement

The ongoing demands on the chief executive officer (CEO) or president in developing an effective quality improvement system represent an enormous personal commitment of time. The CEO must be a champion of the concept of CQI. The CEO must "walk the talk." That is, the CEO must be visible and should take every opportunity to visit various departments and "talk up" the need for quality improvement. Dr. Curt Reimann, Director of the Malcom Baldrige National Quality Award, offers seven key leadership indicators for CEOs and senior executives:[6]

- **Indicator #l: Visibility, commitment, and being knowledgeable**
- **Indicator #2: Missionary zeal**
- **Indicator #3: Aggressive targets**
- **Indicator #4: Strong drivers**
- **Indicator #5: Communication of values**
- **Indicator #6: Organization**
- **Indicator #7: Customer contact**

The CEO should look for someone who has done something right or someone who gone out of his or her way to satisfy a customer and then reward the effort. It is equally important to publicize what happened so that everyone will understand the importance of improving quality.

Leadership and Culture Change

In a recent analysis of organizational culture change, Edgar Schein has identified the fact that leadership is intertwined with the formation, evolution, transformation, and destruction of culture.[7] Culture is created by the actions of leaders; it is also embedded and strengthened by leaders. When culture becomes dysfunctional, leadership is needed to help the group "unlearn" some of its cultural assumptions and learn new ones. Schein believes that such transformation requires what amounts to deliberate and conscious destruction of cultural elements, and it is this aspect of cultural dynamics that makes the leadership tasks both important and difficult to define.

Let's examine the roles of leadership more closely to see what is needed at each stage of development. The leader is the ultimate driver in any organizational change because the leader determines the future. To be successful, today's leaders must utilize five practices:

vision, urgency, empowerment, trust, and **personal responsibility**. These practices, when coupled with the support system role of the quality council, transform management into effective leadership.

The CEO's Role in CQI

The CEO must:

- **Work with employees to decide what the company should be**
- **Focus the quality effort on improving customer service, not cost cutting**
- **Be willing to change**
- **Set up employee problem-solving programs**
- **Work with employees and help them install changes they suggest**
- **Reward employees for improving customer services**
- **Keep employees informed about quality successes**

Now let's continue our journey and see how this transformation can be accomplished. Senior staff and the management team should complete this CQI management development program. It will provide everyone with the background needed for an intelligent discussion of how to install systems to manage your quality improvement efforts.

Monday Morning Mirror Issues

I'll give a speech stressing the importance of high quality.

They heard it before!

Exercise 2

The CEO's Role

Instructions:

The CEO in your firm has expressed a desire for the organization to make whatever cultural changes are necessary for continuous quality improvement. Your assignment is to think through what you would like your CEO to do to either help implement CQI or to help refine the CQI process. Spend ten minutes on this assignment. Work individually to develop four specific written suggestions. Record your suggestions on Worksheet 2.

Develop a written response that completes the thought "Our CEO should..." Then get back together in the main group. Appoint a temporary team leader who will moderate the discussion. Also appoint a scribe who will record the major ideas suggested. Try to reach a general consensus on the top four activities that the CEO should undertake to help with the CQI process.

Worksheet 2

Our CEO

Our CEO should:

The Facilitator's Role in Continuous Quality Improvement

A facilitator is a planner, an organizer, a coach, and a promoter, as well as someone who is willing to encourage the group to discuss issues. You will need a facilitator to lead the discussion in this development program to identify management support systems that will be needed for CQI. It is best that you appoint a facilitator for this series. If possible, this should be the same person who is responsible for guiding the quality improvement process.

That is, it is not absolutely essential that the facilitator for the management development series be the CQI facilitator. However, if they are not the same person, they should at least work closely together in order to ensure continuity of direction as ideas develop.

The ideal facilitator is an unbiased volunteer who does not have a vested interest in the issues discussed. He or she cannot be a key person in management, because employees will assume that there is a hidden agenda in all discussions. The basic rule for a facilitator to follow is to avoid participating in discussions. The facilitator's role is to focus on the process leading to a successful group meeting. Issues of content must be left to the group.

A Facilitator Is:

- **A "neutral" person—he or she should not be a key person in management**
- **A coach, not a player**
- **Someone who encourages ideas from the group and avoids expressing his or her own ideas**
- **A person who plans and guides the flow of the meeting**

The facilitator must plan the topics to be discussed prior to the meeting. The objective to be accomplished during the meeting should be stated at the beginning of each meeting. Then, the facilitator should try to keep the group on track during the meeting. The facilitator does not have to be poised or articulate. In fact, a certain amount of nervousness is to be expected (and natural), especially if the facilitator is attempting to lead a management team. All team members should work with the facilitator in a team spirit and assist in moving the discussion forward. Ask your facilitator to schedule meeting times and locations. All meetings should begin with an explanation of what is to be discussed prior to addressing the scheduled topics.

Problems a Facilitator Will Encounter:

- **Defining top management's role**
- **Keeping the discussion on track**
- **Handling disruptive behavior**
- **Adding closure to meetings**

If your firm is large enough, departmental meetings should be held without the firm's top management in attendance. If the president or a top manager has expressed an interest in participating, be aware that employees are more cautious in their comments when an authoritative figure is present. Remember, in addition to learning about quality improvement, these meetings will help build a quality team by encouraging employees to work together toward common goals. The facilitator should be available if departmental management wants him or her to discuss quality issues with the teams.

Ask the CEO to attend and chair the firm's quality council meetings instead of team meetings designed to solve specific problems. On the other hand, in small firms it may be more natural for teams to deal directly with top management and for top management to attend team meetings.

After a quality council has been created, problem-solving groups will be needed, and the performance of these groups will have to be monitored. The ideal problem-solving group consists of less than six people of similar managerial rank with a cross-sectional mix of skills. For example, a group of clerical employees and a vice-president will probably not be effective. Although groups of all managerial levels will undoubtedly be needed for some tasks, they should be used cautiously.

The Facilitator's Role in CQI

- **Move the process forward**
- **Report to the quality council**
- **Be "neutral" (cannot be a key person in management)**
- **Coach teams, not be a player**
- **Encourage ideas from teams and avoid expressing his or her own ideas**
- **Guide the flow of the meetings**
- **Keep everyone informed**
- **Stay actively involved in CQI**

The two biggest problems confronting a facilitator are how to keep the discussion on track and how to handle disruptive behavior. When conversations get off track or when the same thing has been said time and time again, tell the group: "These are interesting points, but the objective of this meeting is to..." If that doesn't work, tell the group that the topic will be added to a list of open issues to be addressed at a future date.

Handling disruptive behavior, in particular personality clashes, is more difficult. Acknowledge the person's right to express his or her views, but point out that the behavior is disrupting the group. Tell the person(s), "The points you are raising are important, but our time is limited. We need to address the objective of this meeting, which is to..." In summary, perhaps the most important attributes of a facilitator are interpersonal skills and familiarity with the organization.

Exercise 3

The Facilitator's Role

Instructions:

The CEO in your firm has expressed a desire for the organization to make whatever cultural changes are necessary for continuous quality improvement. Your assignment is to think through the characteristics that will be needed by your facilitator. Write these characteristics in the space provided on Worksheet 3. Spend ten minutes on this assignment. Work individually to develop specific written suggestions.

After you have developed a written response that completes the thought "Our facilitator should..." get back together in the main group. Appoint a temporary team leader who will moderate the discussion. Also appoint a scribe who will record the major ideas suggested. Try to reach a general consensus (without voting) on the major characteristics needed by your facilitator.

Worksheet 3

Our Facilitator

Our facilitator should:

Endnotes

1. *The American Heritage Dictionary of the English Language* (3rd Edition), Houghton Mifflin, Boston, 1992.
2. In *Managing for Excellence,* by David Bradford and Allan Cohen (John Wiley & Sons, New York, 1994, pp. 7–10), the notion of the leader as a developer is contrasted with the "heroic" management model of the manager as a controller or director. This work set the stage for the leadership model that is at the core of the continuous quality improvement effort.
3. The Lone Ranger was a fictitious western hero in the early days of television. He would ride into a town to eliminate the outlaws. After putting out a fire, he would leave his trademark, a silver bullet, and ride out of town on his faithful horse, Silver. The problem was that the townspeople were no better able to solve the next problem that came along unless the Lone Ranger came back to help them. Thus, the term heroic management was born.
4. Source: *The Leadership Challenge* by James Kouzes and Barry Posner (Jossey-Bass, San Francisco, 1988).
5. Gooden and English, "Evolution: Quality Means Value," *America's Network,* Quality Supplement, 1994, pp. 32–33.
6. Source: *Total Quality Management,* by Joel Ross (St. Lucie Press, Delray Beach, Fla., 1993, p. 46).
7. Edgar Schein, in his work *Organizational Culture and Leadership* (2nd Edition, Jossey-Bass, San Francisco, 1993), argues that the essential job of leadership in the organization is the manipulation of culture to achieve the desired long-term objectives. As such, the group is always working toward both external survival and the internal integration issues. Schein states that how effectively these issues are addressed is ultimately the function of leadership, in that it is leaders who must, in the end, make the complex calculations of how best to ensure that both sets of issues are addressed.

Chapter 2

Creating a Sense of Urgency

Organizations everywhere are experiencing massive changes such as downsizing in an effort to respond to changing markets and adjust to competitive pressure. Change is a fact of life as many organizations have come to realize that they must make significant changes or run the risk of failure. However, change itself can be a trap. Unless care is exercised by top management, the organization can get so bogged down in the changes that are required to improve short-term effectiveness that it flounders and loses its sense of direction.

The key to mastering and channeling organizational change is to remember that organizations and people do not change unless they see a perceived need to change.[1] While it is the leader's job to create a sense of urgency for change, this must be accomplished by maintaining an optimum stress level within the organization. The driver for change and ultimately for output is stress. Various estimates indicate that 90% of the work gets done in the last 10% of the time available for the work. The problem lies in how managers perceive their roles in creating tension and pressure within the organization

Monday Morning Mirror Issues

Why do I have to spend so much time talking about quality? Can't I just delegate it?

Yes, and that would send a message about how Unimportant it is!

instead of managing the tension. In a "management by control" environment, as output increases on a linear path, so does stress. More stress equals more output in this atmosphere of "yelling and telling" management.[2] Managers who follow this model see their roles as managing deadlines along with the pressure, stress, and things gone wrong. For the most part, trust and open, honest communication decrease as a climate of fear develops and quality of output decreases.

Leaders recognize their job as maintaining and operating on an optimum stress level (or band) within the organization and identifying the critical success factors and core competencies that people must possess in order to perform well in this optimum range. This notion is summed up in the Yerkes–Dobson law of psychology which states that:

> Anxiety improves performance until people reach an optimum motivation level; beyond that point, performance deteriorates as people attain higher anxiety levels.

Organizations that operate in the optimum zone—where stress enhances productivity—are known as highly effective organizations.

Highly effective organizations are led rather than managed. At their core, they are characterized by ten key traits which are built into their value systems, hiring practices, and training, promotion, and reward systems. A sense of urgency governs the development of these traits: **trust, accountability, innovation, leadership, interdependence, risk taking, involvement, teamwork, decision making, motivation,** and **excitement.** Creating a sense of urgency is the first role to be performed by the quality council and can be fostered using a six-initiative support system. The purpose of creating a sense of urgency is to stimulate the organization's thinking toward the implementation of

Monday Morning Mirror Issues

We have to be as concerned about quality --

As we are about budgets and profit.

the CQI transformation model (however that is defined by your organization). At this point in the initiative development plan, the purpose is **not** to develop action items for improvement. It is simply to outline the need for the call to action—and nothing more. Many executives at this point try to develop detail plans for solving the quality problems of their organizations. This will come later in the process as we further develop the roles and initiatives of the council. The purpose of this role is very narrow but extremely important, for without a well-defined and articulated sense of urgency, it is very difficult to break the status quo. The following six core initiatives can be used as a springboard for creating a sense of urgency.

Focus on cost of quality—The cost of quality (COQ) is more accurately referred to as the cost of non-quality or the cost of not doing things right the first time. It has been estimated as anywhere between 20 to 40% of annual sales or revenues. COQ information can be used to inform the organization, in tangible terms, as to how much of company funds are being chewed up by things going wrong. A COQ survey can educate management and all employees about the importance of prevention vs. detection and correction. Survey results can also be used as a benchmark for progress and are a rich source of improvement ideas. A word of caution, however. COQ surveys are not intended to be done on a monthly or even quarterly basis. They are best utilized as one-shot estimates, to be repeated possibly on an annual basis if justified.

Challenge of becoming the best—Becoming number one in your industry or profession and staying there requires a total commitment from the entire organization. The challenge touches upon every employee, every process, and every job. It means implementing continuous improvement in everything we do.

Monday Morning Mirror Issues

Maybe a leader is someone --

Who points you in the right direction, and tells you to get going.

Need for continuous improvement—Fred Smith, founder of Federal Express, sums it up as follows:

> When every employee is involved in improving quality, leaders emerge at every level. It becomes unnecessary to micromanage. The only preconditions are that employees know what is expected from them, know that the organization cares for them, posses the resources to do their jobs, and know they have authority to act. We expect a lot—highly motivated people consciously choosing whatever is in their power to assure every customer is satisfied, and more. Every day!

Dealing with a changing marketplace—All organizations are concerned today with the changing marketplace. The question is when, not if, it will happen. In order to meet the challenges and opportunities, organizations must accelerate the process of becoming more competitive. We must learn to focus on the marketplace as well as the customers. We must create a sense of urgency among all employees to adapt to change in order to survive in the changing marketplace of today and tomorrow.

Competition for jobs—The organization of the future will have fewer positions available, with a higher percentage of educated employees competing for each job. This holds doubly true for senior management positions. The notion of "lifetime employment" is being replaced by "lean and mean" attitudes and strategies that expect the best from everyone. Organizations value speed and superior service above all else. This can lead to healthy competition for jobs, which can be used to create a sense of urgency.

Endnotes

1. According to Robert Reid, founder and director of the Center for Organizational Effectiveness at George Washington University, the leader's role is to communicate the urgency and need for change throughout the organization. In a recently published article entitled "There's More to Quality Management than TQM" (*Quality Digest,* May 1994, pp. 67–70), Reid argues for the creation of the sense of urgency as the number one priority for leadership and the council as well.
2. Ibid. Don Norden and Robert Reid have developed an interesting comparison of the two opposite-pole models of "management by fear" (high stress) and "management by cookies and carrots" (low stress). In the real world, both are seen by Reid and Norden to be ineffective.

Exercise 4

Creating Your Own Sense of Urgency

Instructions:

Every organization needs to create its own sense of urgency based on its own unique conditions and circumstances, which determine its own "proof of need." Remember that each employee has three basic questions around which the leader can effectively frame a sense of urgency:

1. What is expected of me?
2. What's in it for me (WIIFM)?
3. Where do I go with a problem?

Using the information discussed in this chapter and Worksheet 4, it is time to develop your own sense of urgency. Working individually, take fifteen minutes to develop your own "proof of need." Then, working in a group, determine the top three or four elements that can frame your own organization's sense of urgency.

After you have developed your own written ideas, get together as a team and spend an additional thirty minutes reaching consensus as a team.

Worksheet 4

Creating a Sense of Urgency

Create your own proof of need for a renewed sense of urgency:

Chapter 3

Establishing Direction

Introduction

Multiple activities are involved in establishing direction for continuous quality improvement. These activities include creating a long-term vision for the organization, developing a mission statement, developing supporting strategies and guiding principles, aligning key activities, blueprinting (flowcharting), developing measurable targets, reviewing customers and suppliers, prioritizing quality improvements, developing operating plans, and finally, installing the Act-Plan-Do-Check cycle. First, attention is directed toward establishing vision and mission statements.

Monday Morning Mirror Issues

Why emphasize planning? We can't direct the competitive winds.

True, but we can adjust our sails, and try a new tack.

Creating a Vision Statement

Vision defines what we want to be.

The vision is the desired future state of the organization and can be formulated in the context of a vision statement. However, envisioning the future is not the same as predicting what will actually occur in the competitive environment. Envisioning consists of brainstorming general conditions that are likely to occur in the future and then exercising boldness in defining what we (the organization) want to be.

A well-written vision statement provides a sense of direction to guide an organization through numerous changes. The leader who is a visionary can create a self-fulfilling prophecy in that others will have a sense of direction to help make the vision come true. A vision statement should:

- **Be brief**
- **Inspire**
- **Challenge**
- **Describe an ideal condition**
- **Appeal to employees and stockholders**
- **Provide a direction for the future state of the organization**

Monday Morning Mirror Issues

Why are meaningful vision statements difficult?

Because you are trying to create a visual picture.

Many organizations, such as health care organizations, educational organizations, and volunteer groups, are in "natural" industries which permit them to develop powerful vision and mission statements relatively easily. For example, a vision statement for a health care organization might be

To provide for the health and well being of our people

This is a powerful statement. When accompanied by a mission statement such as

Our business is saving lives

it adds a focus that motivates and guides the organization.

Ford Motor Company has a no-nonsense vision:

...to be the maker of the highest quality cars and trucks in the world

In other words, Ford plans on being the best.

One way to develop a vision statement for your organization is for the executive team to participate in an exercise. For example, suppose that reporters from *Business Week* and *The Wall Street Journal* are interviewing your company five years from now. They want you to write the lead paragraph for their articles. In the lead paragraph (written five years from now), what can you say about your organization? What does it do? Who are its customers?

Write the major themes that are represented in the different paragraphs on a flip chart. Then craft a vision statement with these ideas as a course of action. Think in terms of headings and subheadings as an aid in organizing your thoughts in order to develop a vision that everyone can "buy into."

Mission statements are not designed to "nail everything down." In fact, some vagueness is desirable. Concentrate on developing a general direction, an image, and a general philosophy to guide the organization.

Mission Statement

Mission defines the core purpose of being in terms of the accomplishments needed that will result in realization of the vision.

A vision without a mission statement is often a pipe dream. A mission statement describes the core purpose of being and the accomplishments that are necessary to move the organization toward its vision. A mission statement addresses those factors that are necessary to realize the vision. That is, a mission statement addresses the achievements needed in major areas of importance to the organization.

A mission statement is often the most visible part of a strategic plan. A good mission statement should include all of the essential components of the future thrust of the organization. It should also communicate a positive feeling that will guide others to action. The vision and philosophy can be included in the mission statement or can be stated separately.

Key Components of a Mission Statement:

Core purpose	What is the organization's bread-and-butter reason for being that distinguishes it from others?
Customers	Who are the customers of the organization?
Markets	Where does the organization compete geographically?
Products or services	What are the major products or services?
Technology	What is the organization's basic technology?
Economic goals	What is the organization's attitude toward growth and profitability?

Self-concept	What are the organization's strengths and competitive advantage?
Image	What public image is desired?
Philosophy	What are the fundamental beliefs and values?
Effectiveness	Does the mission statement address the wishes of key stakeholders?
Inspiration	Does the statement motivate people?

There is no single, generic mission statement for all organizations, nor do all mission statements have to be lengthy. Differences will occur, but perhaps the key point is that an effective mission statement specifies the fundamental reason why an organization exists. In doing so, it provides guidance for the strategic plan.

Quality Mission Statement

A statement from the company on what it wants to be in five years.

It should communicate guiding principles and values held by the organization.

Objectives:

- **Show the direction of the firm at a future point in time**
- **A tool to position the customers' perceptions about the company and to improve the firm's image**
- **A guide to each part of the company to use in creating its own specific quality objectives**

Guiding Principles

The vision statement is what we want to be, while the mission statement identifies what needs to be accomplished in the key areas that affect our business. The gap between the two will undoubtedly be difficult for some people to accept. Guiding principles help bridge the gap by identifying the fundamental, underlying beliefs that guide our actions. Many Malcolm Baldrige National Quality Award winners, as well as companies that have successfully completed ISO 9000 certification, have stated that without employees working together in empowered work groups, the organization would not have been successful in its pursuit of improved quality or ISO 9000 certification.

In other words, an underlying belief in basic human values is needed in order for an organization to come together. Beliefs such as treating customers and employees with respect, dignity, and honesty cannot be mere words; they must guide actions.

Summary

Clear vision and mission statements, along with a statement of organizational beliefs, provide the basis by which departments can focus their quality improvement efforts. Make sure your organization not only has meaningful vision and mission statements, but that such statements are communicated to your employees.

Monday Morning Mirror Issues

How can I get people to like change?

You can't get them to like change. Promote the reality: Change is inevitable, survival is optional.

Exercise 5

AT&T's Vision

Instructions:

Read the following excerpt (from *Business Week,* August 30, 1993) about AT&T. Then write your vision and mission statements for AT&T in the space provided in Worksheet 5. Spend fifteen minutes on this, and then get together in teams to discuss your ideas. Appoint a new team leader to lead the discussion, and try to reach a general consensus (without voting) on the major topics. We will then get together to discuss the different approaches.

Recommended reading: John Pearce and Fred Davis, "Corporate Mission Statements: The Bottom Line." *Academy of Management Executive,* 1987, Vol. 1, No. 2, pp. 109–116.

Background:

AT&T, with $68 billion in 1993 sales, just purchased the largest cellular phone company, McCaw Cellular Communications. AT&T paid heavily for their late entry into the cellular phone market. The cost was $12.6 billion for McCaw's stock, and AT&T is assuming $5 billion in McCaw debt. Their purchase of McCaw is approximately $300 per potential subscriber, making it one of the most expensive cellular buyouts ever.

The specter of a nationwide cellular phone service has competitors nervous. AT&T is banking that the purchase of McCaw could be a boon to their bottom line as they find a way to link cellular customers directly to their long-distance networks, bypassing local phone systems. This will reduce the $14 billion a year AT&T currently pays to local phone companies (called Baby Bells). AT&T will then be able to proceed with building a network spanning the globe and fill that network with every kind of communication, including voice, data, video, computer, and entertainment.

Some insiders called the deal "gutsy"; others felt AT&T has finally overextended themselves. Even AT&T's chairman Robert Allen concedes this is a risky deal. The AT&T–McCaw link will give Baby Bells the argument they need to sway regulators to let them enter long-distance services, particularly if they give up their monopolies in local service.

So AT&T is taking a calculated risk: they could lose the savings if the Baby Bells are granted the right to enter the long-distance market. However, insiders agree that the McCaw deal will increase AT&T's business outside the US. Allen hopes to increase internal revenues from 25% to 40% of the total business in the next five years. Cellular service is particularly popular in developing countries such as China, which can utilize cellular technology to modernize their phone service far more rapidly than with wired systems. In the developed countries in Europe, most regulations do not apply to cellular, affording AT&T a large advantage over local phone companies.

There is also a possibility that a new wireless system called Personal Communications Service (PCS) will emerge as a major rival to cellular phones. Cellular networks use powerful transmitters to relay signals across towers 20 miles apart. The PCS territory is far smaller, and since callers are closer to transmitters, the handsets need less power, making them smaller and cheaper, and they have a longer battery life. Furthermore, the small territories enable PCS systems to carry a greater communication capability, making the per-call cost more economical, which should attract more customers.

Additionally, the Federal Communications Commission (FCC) is considering regulation that will increase competitors in the market. That means that if PCS is the dominant communication medium of the future, major investments will be needed by AT&T in the cellular network purchased from McCaw to install numerous transmitters. For example, a PCS network to cover Chicago will require 200 cells (towers and relays) at a cost of $250,000 per cell.

Allen says he and his staff have considered all the arguments and agonized over the purchase decision. Not all major purchase decisions have gone well for AT&T. Sun Microsystems, Inc. and Olivetti cost billions in investment but have produced little in the way of revenue. Allen agrees not all purchases were wise, and has since divested the majority of non-communications business. AT&T must make this purchase "work" if they are to be a viable firm in the next century.

Worksheet 5

AT&T's Vision

Ideas for AT&T's vision and mission statements:

Exercise 6

The Reporter

Instructions:

It is five years in the future and a reporter from *The Wall Street Journal* has just contacted you. He is writing a story about your organization and has asked you to write the lead paragraph for the article. What special aspects of your firm will capture their readers' attention?

Spend the next fifteen minutes privately developing at least three key ideas. Use Worksheet 6 to record your ideas. This is a very important exercise. Be as innovative as possible. Don't worry about practicalities; we are after breakthrough ideas. Be prepared to share your thought-provoking ideas.

After you have developed your own written ideas, get together in teams. Appoint a new team leader (in fact, rotate team leadership for each exercise) to guide the discussion, and try to reach a general consensus (without voting) on the major topics that you would tell the reporter. Rank the topics from most important to least important. Spend an hour on this exercise.

After your team reaches a general consensus on the ideas to tell the reporter, develop consensus on a general ranking of the ideas. Then meet with the other teams and share your ideas. Appoint a scribe (a recorder) who will keep track of the major ideas, as well as **why** people felt the ideas were important.

Do **not** attempt to reach a consensus at this point. You need time to think and to develop new ideas. The scribe should distribute a written copy of the ideas and a brief explanation of why the ideas were deemed important, without reference to the team or group that offered the idea. Then, after completion of this management development program, hold another meeting to discuss the ideas.

After completion of this development program, and when you have what you feel are "working" mission and vision statements, solicit ideas and suggestions from all employees. It is recommended that you distribute your written ideas. Then hold departmental meetings to discuss the proposed vision and to solicit suggestions.

Worksheet 6

The Reporter

Ideas to discuss with the reporter:

Chapter 4

Supporting Strategies and Guiding Principles

Vision and mission statements that describe the current and future state of the organization do not become reality simply because a group of people wrote them down. Change will undoubtedly be required, but if people feel that they are going to be terminated as a result of the change or that there are is a hidden agenda which will result in a loss of power, then change will be resisted.

A guiding principle is a basic truth that can be immediately practiced. For example, treating every employee as an associate who deserves to be treated with respect, honesty, and dignity may sound trite, but without it, you cannot achieve a high-performance organization. A worthy vision must be guided by worthy principles that express and enact fundamental core values. These core values include factors such as trust, honesty, truth, integrity, respect, loyalty, and faithfulness.

If these values are installed, then employees will have the confidence to make decisions without fear of reprisal in the event something goes wrong. Furthermore, employees can be empowered to inspect their own work (build in quality) and to take corrective action without constantly seeking approval from higher managerial levels. Some examples of guiding principles have been chosen from the American Society for Quality Control (ASQC) Education Division.

Serving the Customer

Serving the customer must become the central priority around which all other activity revolves. The idea of customer-focused strategies must begin with the ASQC Education Division. The very notion of having customers is alien to most campuses. Considering students as customers is perceived by many faculty as relegating themselves to the position of being employees, and the notion of being a customer-driven organization must become more highly regarded. The Education Division must become a model for educators to follow, both in practice and in dissemination of theory.

Continuous Improvement

Continuous improvement of the system of education must become a way of life and must start with us. The process of continuous improvement is dependent upon learning new skills and practicing these skills on small, achievable projects which collectively push toward attainment of the vision and mission. It is the application of the Deming/Shewhart cycle of improvement to all areas of the system of education.

Monday Morning Mirror Issues

What is an innovative, long-term quality goal?

To be the benchmark that others try to meet.

Speaking with Facts

Speaking with facts must become one of the principal aims of the system of education, including the ASQC. The underlying purpose of this principal is to forever and always aim quality at the needs and wants of the customer, both present and future. To this end, various fact-gathering tools must be learned and mastered. The ASQC must take a leadership role, and a pioneering effort must be encouraged and rewarded.

Respect for People

Respect for people will become a way of life for everyone and anything involved in the quality system of education. This means that everyone must be involved and empowered, from the top to the bottom, and respect and trust promoted and valued. Dr. Deming would often devote a majority of lecture time to this principle, and eight of his Fourteen Points tie into this principle.

Transformation

The transformation of the system of education and the organizations involved is required for lasting change. A new attitude is required in order to create a new culture that focuses on the continuous improvement of systems and educational services in order to become truly customer-obsessed.

Partnerships

Partnerships with suppliers and the community is one of the marks of the enlightened educational organization. The extended enterprise of the organization of the future sees suppliers and the external community as partners in the system of providing quality educational products and services.

Value-Added Services

Cost-effective, value-added services are essential to success. To accomplish the mission and vision, educational organizations need to add value-laden services to compete in the "global village" of tomorrow.

Monday Morning Mirror Issues

I've got it --

Quality isn't negotiable!

Exercise 7

The Pesky Reporter

Instructions:

The time is five years from now, and yesterday you had a discussion with a reporter from *The Wall Street Journal,* who took a lot of notes regarding the accomplishments of your organization. It is 9:00 a.m. and the reporter is waiting for you at your office. You ask him what he wants. He smiles, thanks you for your previous assistance, and asks:

- What are the most important guiding principles and values that your employees hold regarding your organization?
- What did you do in the past five years to bring about an acceptance of these values?
- After a new employee's first month on the job, what will he or she feel are the two most important characteristics of your firm?

Spend fifteen minutes developing your response to the reporter's questions. Record your answers on Worksheet 7.

After you have developed your own written ideas, get together in teams. Appoint a new team leader to guide the discussion, and try to reach a general consensus (without voting) on the ideas that you would tell the reporter. Rank the topics from most important to least important. Spend thirty minutes on this, and then get together as a group and discuss the ideas.

Worksheet 7

That Pesky Reporter

Future value ideas:

Quality Objectives

A mission statement provides a general sense of direction, and departmental objectives should assist in accomplishing the organization's overall mission. One possible format for departmental objectives is shown on the next page (we're concentrating on quality objectives).

A management team should feel free to develop its own format. However, whatever format is decided upon should then be followed by all departments.

Monday Morning Mirror Issues

What is so important about a mission statement?

Where do you want to go with the organization?

Format of Quality Objectives

Departments must develop specific, measurable objectives that contribute to the mission statement

Form: To [action—increase/decrease/improve] what [product or service] by [date]

Example:

Wrong: To increase customer quality in our department

Right: To increase customer quality in our department by 10% by January 1, 1995.

To sensitize company employees regarding quality control:

- Have all supervisors attend a quality workshop by January 1
- Appoint a CQI facilitator by June 1
- Select a test department for CQI by September 1

Exercise 8

Developing Departmental Quality Objective

Instructions:

Using the tentative mission statement previously developed as a guide, select a department and use Worksheet 8 to outline the departmental quality objectives. Take about fifteen minutes to complete this exercise. Be prepared to share your top three objectives with the group.

Remember, this exercise is based on a tentative mission statement. Do not rush the process and accept the mission statement as a usable, final version. At this point in the process, you are only trying to develop an idea as to how things fit together. An important piece is missing from this jigsaw puzzle: after completion of this workbook, you will have to identify the organizational structure needed to facilitate meeting the mission and vision of your organization.

Worksheet 8

Developing Objectives

Departmental quality objectives:

Chapter 5

The Quality Council: A Structure for Continuous Quality Improvement

A quality council (sometimes called a steering committee or executive committee) provides a formal structure for an organization's quality improvement efforts. It is the leadership structure of the organization and consists of at least two (or more) interlocking levels within the organizational framework. The **executive quality council** is the highest level and consists of the president/CEO, direct-reporting vice-presidents, and other members appointed by the president. Its charter includes developing policy to create, foster, and continuously improve all aspects of the quality system.

The second level, called the **local area quality council**, is composed of senior management who oversee the various cross-functional task teams and assist in keeping the organization focused on Continuous Quality Improvement (CQI).

The structure of a typical quality council is depicted on the next page. A senior member of the executive committee (such as the president or executive vice-president) should chair the council, which is normally composed of department managers.

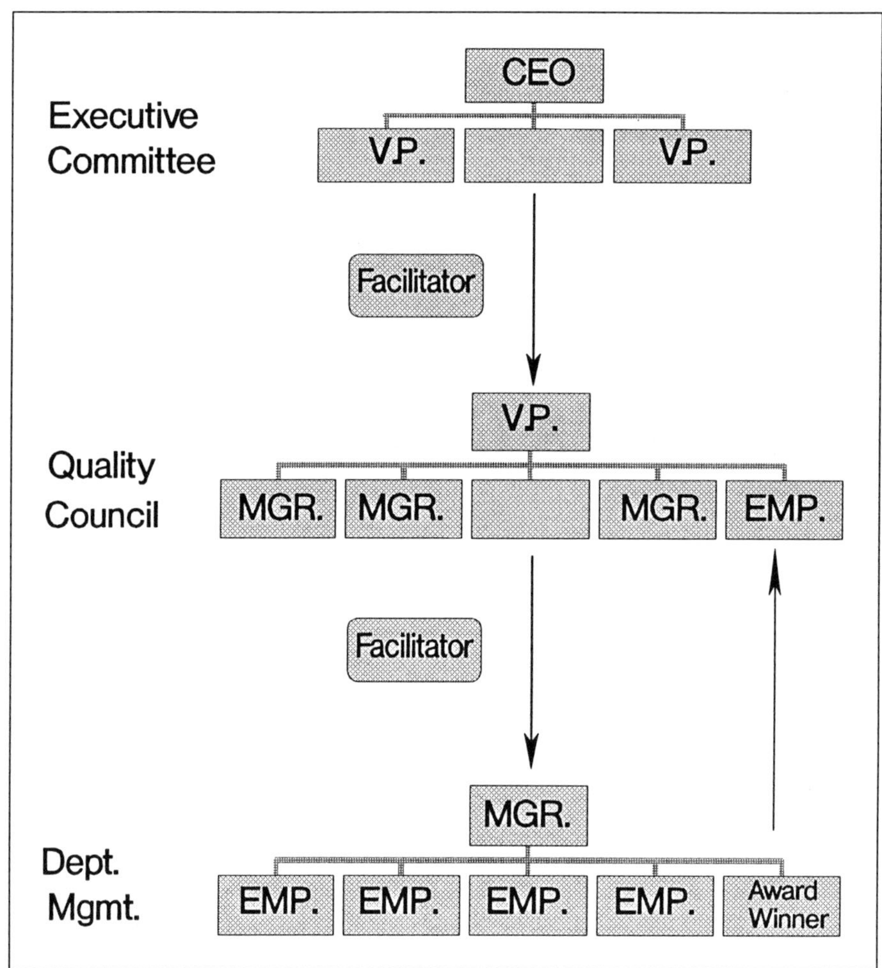

Typical Quality Council

This arrangement provides the formal structure needed to select projects, assign and assist quality improvement teams, and follow up on implementation. Without the formal structure provided by a council comprised of top management, quality ideas are typically discussed and then put on the back burner because most good ideas cut across functional lines.

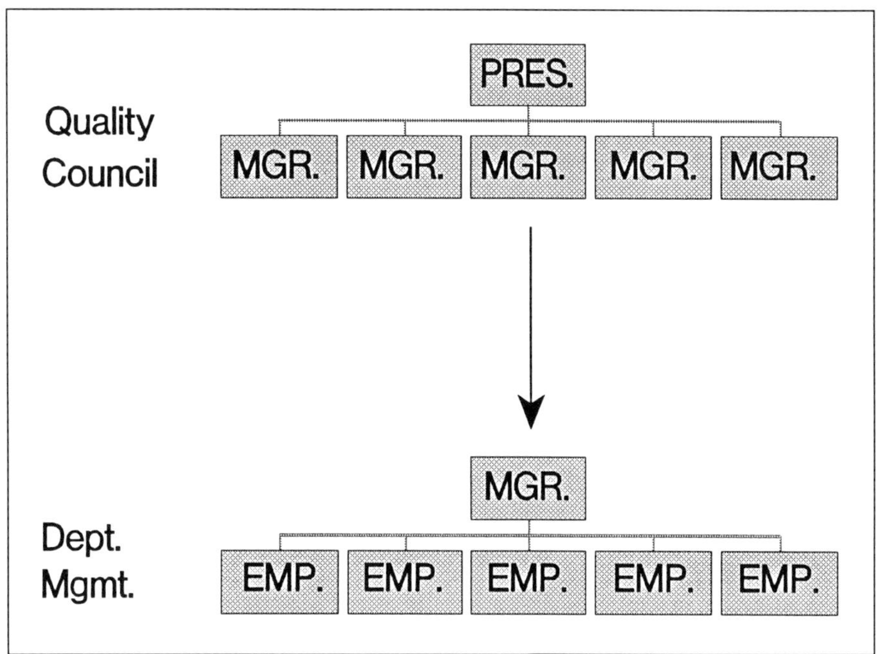

Quality Council in Small Organizations

Smaller firms may have a more tightly knit management group, where each manager in turns chairs a quality council in his or her own department. This can be very effective, but care should be taken to ensure that the various groups do not become too large and unwieldy. Each council is charged with establishing an environment in which quality will be improved and sustained, providing the leadership and personal involvement to guide CQI in the organization, and developing its own continuous improvement plan that will enable it to carry out its charge.

A facilitator is often assigned to coordinate the various quality teams, particularly in larger firms. This coordination role is a time-consuming process, and what begins as a part-time job quickly grows into a full-time job for a facilitator. Ideally, a facilitator should possess both technical quality improvement skills and human relations/team-building skills in order to be able to provide assistance to teams as needed.

Quality Council: Facilitator's Role

Focus on making CQI a reality

- Work with managers
- Recommend quality procedures
- Assist council
- Coordinate sessions

Conduct CQI training

Work with groups in CQI implementation

Tap basic motivators

- Frustration: the system demotivates
- Need for recognition
- Department management: opportunity to demonstrate potential

A good facilitator is a believable alternative

- He or she is someone you can talk to
- Gets dialogue going between groups
- Keeps the process moving ahead

The problem most organizations face is not in getting employees to offer improvement ideas, but rather in providing assistance in implementing ideas. It is not the technical difficulties that will be problematic for teams to overcome; it is the turf battles and power plays. A council that is openly alert to these barriers can work closely with the teams to remove such obstacles.

Quality Council Needs

There is no problem in identifying improvement ideas

Quality ideas are discussed and then put on the back burner because:

- Problems are not placed on an authoritative agenda
- There was no clear responsibility assigned to solve the problem
- It was not realized that a team was required

A structure is needed to

- Choose projects
- Assign responsibility
- Follow up on implementation

After the council becomes established and has assisted teams in installing concepts that cross functional lines, employee representation on the council can help the various teams understand that the role of the council is to provide authoritative assistance when needed. Employee membership can take the form of a two-month rotating position given to an employee as recognition for an outstanding contribution to the organization's quality improvement effort.

Monday Morning Mirror Issues

Why does Tom resist change in his department?

Because change is threatening and his authority is being reduced.

Successful Quality Councils

It is not unusual to find an organization that has a quality council, but it is unusual to find a council that is successful in implementing and directing the organization's CQI efforts. There are many reasons for this lack of success, but the primarily reason is that quality councils are often composed of a group of executives who are used to operating autonomously.

A successful quality council must be an executive team that works together to improve quality. The council is not a get-together of strong-willed people to "hammer out" agreements. The council must have a clearly defined function, it must have the personal commitment of the CEO, it should be chaired by senior management, and it must be comprised of management from the major departments in the organization.

An effective quality council is one whose members have helped to create a sense of urgency, as well as establish the direction (mission, vision, and strategies/objectives, as discussed earlier) of the organization. They have a shared vision of the future of the organization. Council members **must** be willing to change. They cannot take the attitude that they are defending their home turf or representing particular vested interests. Employees will quickly recognize political alliances. If a particular group repeatedly exercises inflexibility, enthusiasm will be lost.

After a quality council has been formed and procedures have been developed, the typical council will tackle CQI in phases. Phase I can easily take six months of just working with department management to develop a commitment and engagement to quality improvement. Phase II consists of working with and training department managers in CQI techniques. After management is comfortable with the techniques and has an idea of what to expect, a test department can be selected. Then, in Phase III, employees in the test department are trained and quality improvement teams are established. Finally, in Phase IV, a year or two may be required to scale up the quality improvement process across the organization.

Quality Council: Phases

Phase I: Six Months

- Work with department management
- Conduct CQI for department management
- Select projects with dollar savings

Phase II: Three Months

- Department management training in CQI

Phase III: Six Months

- Test department employees' involvement
- Conduct CQI training
- Balance meaning vs. dollar savings

Phase IV: One to Two Years

- Scale up across the firm
- Train all employees
- Select meaningful projects

CQI is not a simple concept, nor is the role of the quality council as straightforward as one might think. For example, suppose Ajax Manufacturing Company specializes in high-volume production, produced to exacting customer specifications. Ajax is profitable and sales are satisfactory, but a quality improvement team thinks that there is a better way of doing business. Senior marketing people (technically competent in the products Ajax is producing) call on key accounts on a routine basis. When these key accounts are engaged in prototyping (creating a new product), Ajax salespeople integrate themselves closely with the firms' buyers and designers.

A quality improvement team recommends that minor customer changes could be noted by Ajax senior sales representatives on engineering documentation which they carry. The team recognizes that the changes would have to be limited in scope and would not substitute for permanent engineering. The quality improvement team finds qualified and willing manufacturing hourly employees who can produce to this documentation (which would be faxed to them), without sacrificing quality, and then send the revised part back to the customer by air delivery. That is, changes would not first be sent to engineering to upgrade their documentation. Nor would the revised engineering document be sent to manufacturing engineering for tool and machine specification. Nor would production control schedule the changes. Nor would material control order the needed material (for one thing, there is no updated bill of material). Nor would quality control inspect the material or finished product. Nor would the part be sent via inside transportation to shipping to be routed to the customer in a standardized manner.

What would happen is that a skilled, senior-level machinist would call a local steel supply house for immediate delivery of the material needed, produce the prototype, and then call a local overnight shipper to pick up the part as soon as it is available. The payoff for key customers when they are developing prototype products prior to volume production is a reduction in turnaround time from three weeks to three days. Because Ajax would be involved in the product from inception of the idea, it will be the preferred supplier.

How would a typical director of engineering react to the quality improvement team's proposal, which virtually removes the engineering department from the design loop? Would he or she place ob-

Monday Morning Mirror Issues

That team idea is a good one. Why can't they install it?

Because changes are required and the team does not have the authority.

stacles in the path of this innovative proposal? When it was actually time to implement the proposal, would the director of manufacturing and the director of quality really permit such empowerment? Would production control allow a machinist to "bump" schedules, even if for a few hours? Would purchasing permit an hourly employee to order material directly?

The effectiveness of a quality council is determined by how it handles suggestions that cross functional lines. A moment's though on this example can identify dozens of valid reasons why such a change could not be accomplished, but only one reason why Ajax should install the proposal: its customers want it.

Membership on a quality council must be viewed as an opportunity for members to bring about change. The importance of the tone established by the senior chair of the committee cannot be overemphasized. A council that works together as a team and adopts a positive "we can make this new idea work" attitude sends a message to all members of the organization: your ideas really count.

Standardizing Input

Employees often have difficulty explaining their quality improvement ideas to others. Some difficulties are understandable, as many improvement ideas deal with subjective quality attributes. Unfortunately, most communication difficulties can be attributed to technical people trying to impress others with their knowledge by using acronyms and jargon peculiar to their area. The result of such communication is that no one outside of that department can understand the suggestion for improvement.

Proposals must be clearly communicated so that the quality council can make intelligent decisions regarding improvement projects and so that success stories can be publicized. One way to obtain understandable input is to ask all quality improvement teams to present their proposals in the form of a graphic **continuous quality improvement story**.

Quality Council: Standardize Input

Structure for quality improvement

Quality improvement story approach

- Standardize input
- Communication tool
- Utilizes proven quality improvement tools

Five-step process

- Reason for improvement
- Current situation
- Analysis
- Implementation plan
- Results

Conduct CQI training

- Employee training required

All CQI stories follow the five quality improvement steps. Whenever possible, each step should be described on a single page.

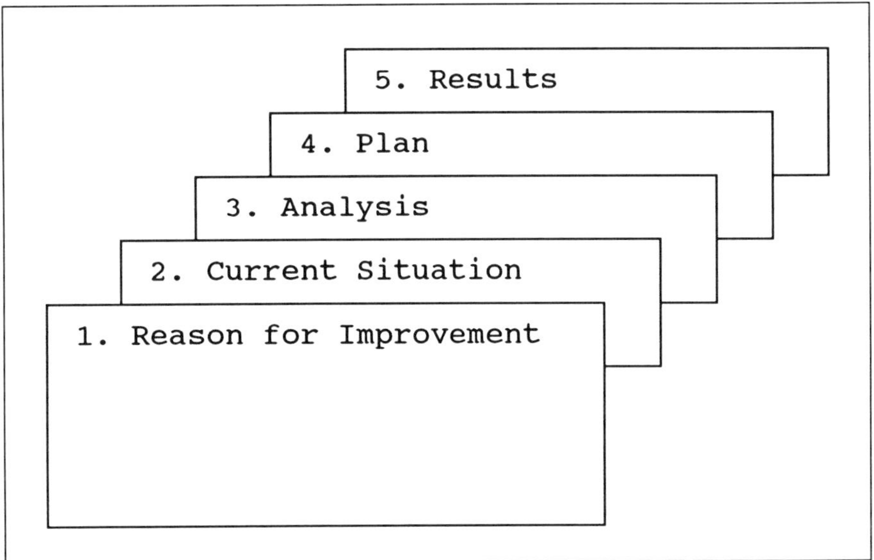

The objective of the first step, **reason for improvement**, is to identify a theme (problem area) and a problem statement. This can be as simple as shown below.

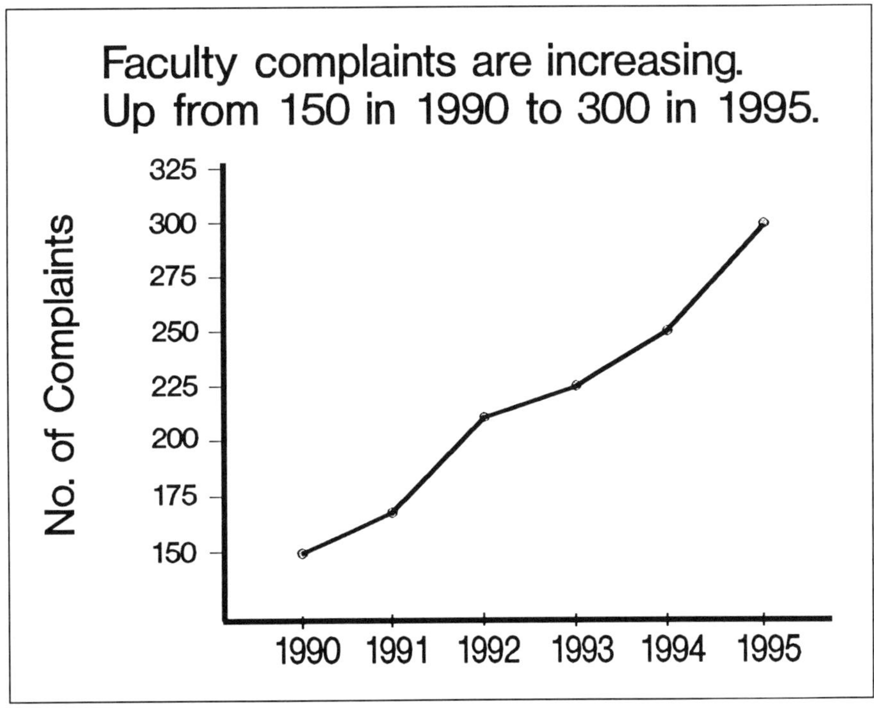

Step 1: Reason for Improvement

The second step, **the current situation**, breaks down the broad theme into its component parts and identifies which component part has the largest impact.

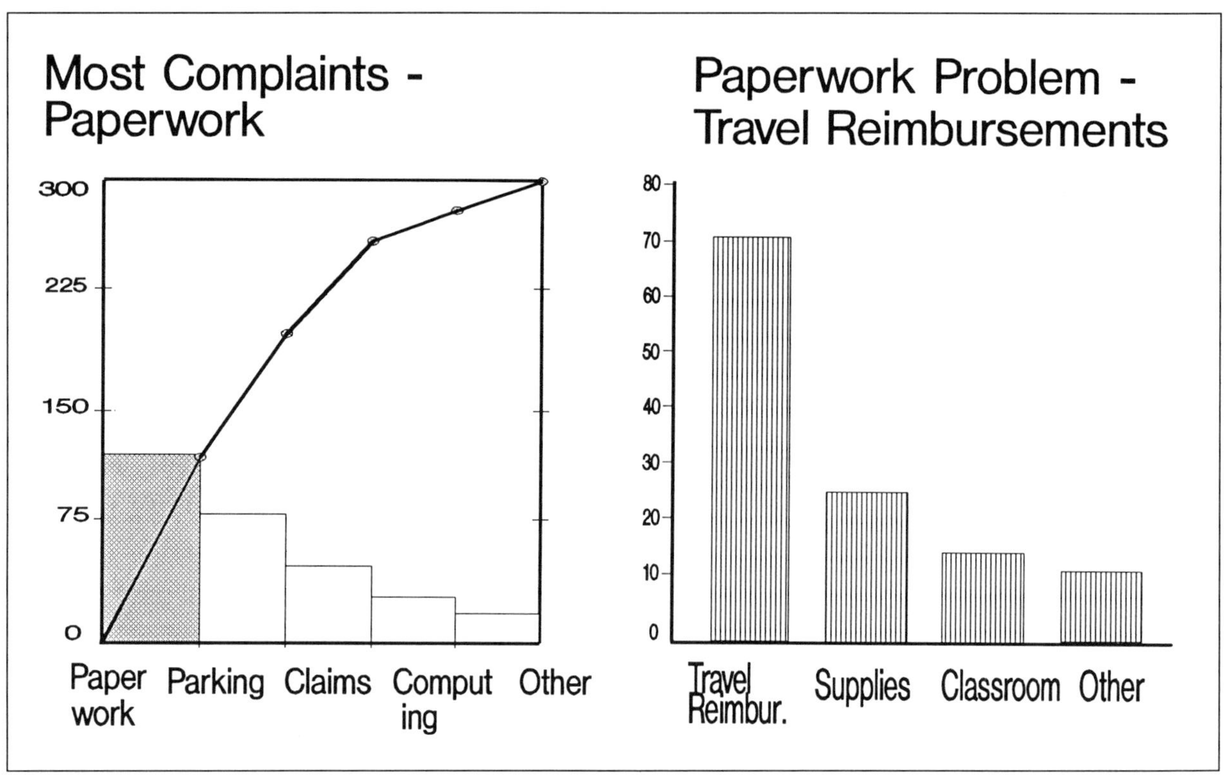

Step 2: Current Situation

The third step is a **summary of the analysis**, which identifies the root cause(s) of the problem.

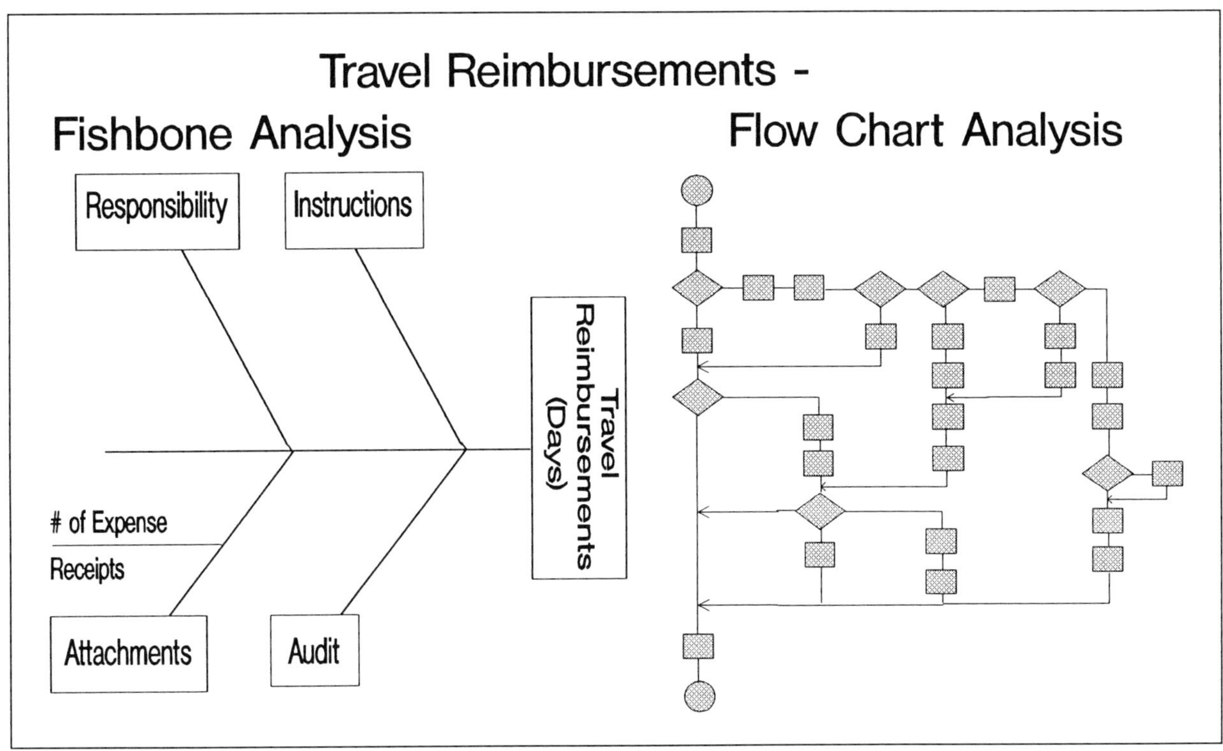

Step 3: Analysis

The fourth step is the **action plan**, which contains an outline of how the CQI team proposes correcting the root cause of the problem. This plan consists of a series of brief statements specifying the exact action to be taken.

What	When	Who	Status
Barriers to Overcome -			
Train secretaries	2/15	Deans	Started
Standardize forms	4/15	Auditing	Completed
Train accountants	5/15	Acc. Dept.	Unknown
Other Assignments -			
Develop tracking program	2/15	MIS Dept.	Not Started

Step 4: Action Plan

Results are reported after the quality improvement team installs the changes. This simple, brief graphic summary typically consists of a before and after condition.

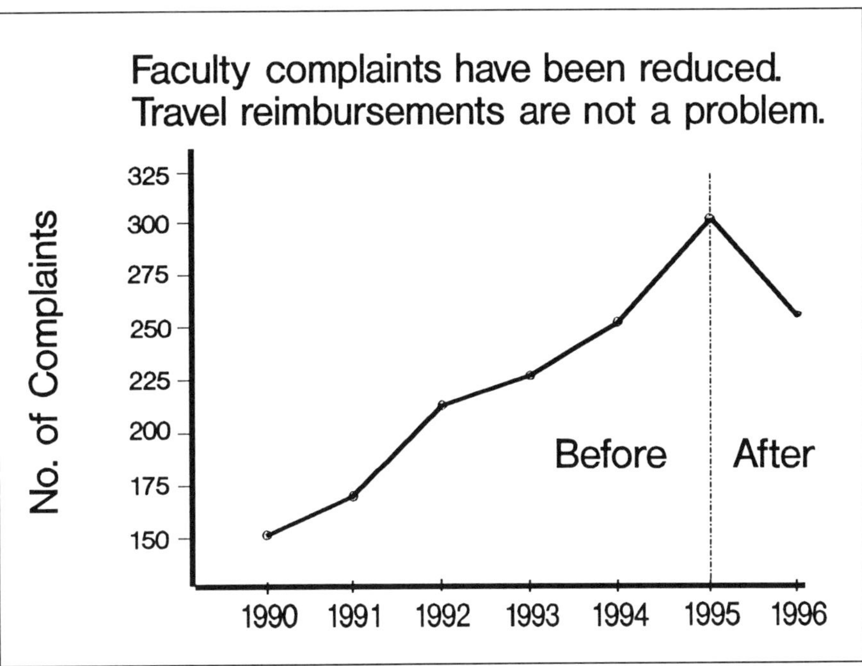

Step 5: Results

For an excellent discussion of how to increase the effectiveness of a quality council, read "Planning for Successful Steering Committees" by Dan Ciampa (*Journal for Quality and Participation,* December 1992, pp. 22–34).

The story approach for reporting quality improvements originated with Dr. Kume. This approach formed the basis of a seven-step quality reporting process used by Florida Power and Light (FPL). The five-step CQI story used in this book is a simplification of FPL's approach. For a complete description of the CQI story and how to achieve quality improvement, read *Quality Improvement Tools and Techniques* by Peter Mears (McGraw-Hill, New York, 1995).

Monday Morning Mirror Issues

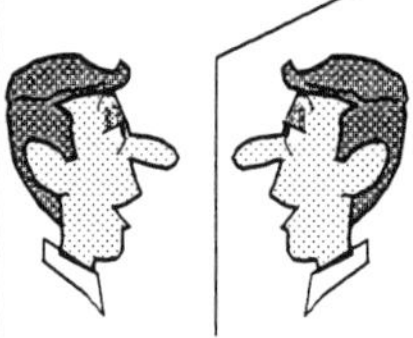

TQM - Total Quality Mayhem!

When executives and employees are out of sync.

Exercise 9

It's a Good Idea—Just Do It!

Instructions:

The president of Ajax Corporation receives a copy of the team's report on how to improve customer response time during prototyping. The report specifies changes required in the way marketing, manufacturing, and engineering work together. The president calls the quality improvement team into his office and tells them: "It's a good idea—just do it! See me if there are any problems."

Break up into small groups of four to five people. Brainstorm what is likely to occur when the quality improvement team attempts to install the proposal. Also, identify how you would envision that a quality council could assist the team. Appoint the least senior person to serve as team leader. Take 30 minutes to develop a brief written outline of the major points. Record your ideas on Worksheet 9. Be prepared to discuss and defend your points with the group.

Worksheet 9

It's a Good Idea—Just Do It!

What might happen when a team tries to install the proposal? How could a quality council assist the team?

Chapter 6

Roles of a Successful Quality Council

The questions confronting a quality council that is trying to sustain a Continuous Quality Improvement (CQI) movement are formidable. We will tackle this problem in terms of the major initiatives that are performed by the quality council. Overall, there are seven major initiatives that the council performs, once the renewed sense of urgency has been created and the direction aligned. In this chapter, we will deal with the support systems for four of these initiatives:

- **Demonstrating personal commitment**
- **Sponsoring teams and providing resources**
- **Coaching and communicating**
- **Employee involvement**

In Chapter 7, we will discuss the support systems needed for reporting and evaluating quality results as well as the payoff initiative of recognizing and rewarding. In Chapter 8, we will discuss how to continue to engage, encourage, and empower. Chapter 9 will deal with understanding the consumer, while Chapter 10 will cover the integrative initiative of developing the measurement system.

Demonstrating Personal Commitment

In a parable about a country breakfast, the chicken was overheard talking about commitment. "I work so hard every day providing eggs for the farmer's breakfast!" she exclaimed. After a long silence, the pig was heard to reply, "My dear, you are only occasionally involved. With me, it is a lifetime commitment!"

There are nine core elements for the council to consider in the support system for the initiative of demonstrating personal commitment. Of all the initiatives that senior management must successfully undertake, perhaps none is more powerful or transformational than a leader with commitment. The following support structures should be considered.

Sponsor teams and attend team meetings—Once a decision to form teams has been made, every team needs to be sponsored by a member of the quality council. Among other things, the sponsor needs to be available, visible, and involved. This means attending team meetings whenever possible. Setting an example and keeping everyone informed are also appropriate, as discussed in the leadership characteristics found in the earlier chapters.

Track progress on a regular basis—The quality council should keep track of the progress of all the teams under its leadership and share this progress with other members of the organization, as appropriate. Follow-up questions should be asked of team members to demonstrate involvement. The council members also need to keep track of their own progress using quality measures.

Discuss satisfaction levels with customers and suppliers—Doing this effectively often means spending a day or so each week with customers and suppliers, preferably on their turf. "How are we doing?" should be the ongoing question, and discussion needs to be centered around results to date. Focus groups are an excellent method of discussing issues with customer groups.

Make periodic informal visits to work areas—One of the most effective habits a council member can cultivate is that of practicing what Tom Peters calls MBWA—Management By Wandering Around. The term "wandering" emphasizes the informality of the visit. This is the opposite of a planned dog-and-pony show. Bob Galvin, retired chairman of Motorola, kept a "Quality Indicator Card," and one of the indices that he checked off was the various departments that he visited each month. Bob didn't make a big announcement that he was coming. He just did it often!

Attend other council meetings to learn and grow—Often we can learn from others that which we cannot see in ourselves. Try to attend one or two other council meetings, and bring back a couple of good ideas for your own council. This is a form of internal benchmarking. Exemplary companies call this "replication."

Provide plenty of training—In the field of real estate, the key is location, location, location. In the field of total quality, it is training, training, training: training for employees, training for supervisors and managers, and training for senior executives. In many excellent organizations, this training is budgeted and tracked as part of the corporate measurement system. The point is that by providing training on an as-needed basis, the council demonstrates a commitment to furthering excellence throughout the organization.

Champion and sponsor a quality-related initiative—Each council member should sponsor at least one endeavor, whether it involves reducing cycle time, a quality improvement technique, a measurement initiative, or a benchmarking initiative. Taking ownership puts quality improvement on a personal level. It is where the rubber meets the road.

Seek out information and resources on continuous quality improvement—The corporate library and public library are good sources. The question is where to start and how to sift through all the material on a selective basis. The American Society for Quality Control and the Association for Quality and Participation are two organizations that have local chapters, which often are excellent sources of reliable information. The Conference Board has a good, limited supply of various reports on quality. Also, attending a Baldrige-winner Quality Day helps build the information network.

Walk the talk—The bottom line is that what you do and the behaviors you demonstrate are what will ultimately make your quality improvement effort successful. (See "Creating a Vision Statement" in Chapter 3.)

Exercise 10

Strategies for Personal Commitment

Instructions:

Get together in your assigned team and appoint a team leader. Spend ten minutes working individually to identify the initiatives that your team will focus on. Use Worksheet 10 to record your ideas. Be prepared to explain why you feel what you have identified is a key (i.e., critical) quality factor.

Then get together as a team. Your team has thirty minutes to try to reach consensus on the major initiatives and support structures. Limit your reporting requirements to three or four key points that can be used to demonstrate personal commitment. Your team leader will then explain the ideas your team came up with to the larger group.

Worksheet 10

Strategies for Personal Commitment	
Support Systems for Personal Commitment	
Area of Commitment	Specific Actions

Sponsoring Teams and Providing Resources

> There is a standard joke in corporate America that it is tough to stay focused on draining the swamp when you constantly find yourself up to your hips in alligators. Investment in a quality process is an investment in draining the swamp; maintaining the investment is the promise to shareholders, employees, and customers that the alligator population will steadily decrease.
>
> *Joan Gebhardt*

The eye-catching title of the best-selling book *Quality Is Free,* by Phil Crosby, is not deliberately misleading. A quality process consumes resources in several forms. Crosby only means that any quality effort more than pays for itself in the long run. Time is the most obvious investment. Besides its own time, management commits thousands of hours of employee time. By sponsoring a team, we commit the organization's resources. Training in quality methods also requires time. Happily, one of the by-products of improving quality is increased efficiency and effectiveness—which results in a savings of time.

Training as a provided resource is not optional. Depending on the size and experience of the training department, you may choose to either develop your own courses to support the quality process or purchase "off-the-shelf" courses and adapt them as appropriate. As with the development of the process as a whole, care must be taken to ensure that the training courses are perceived to be "owned" by the trainers and the company.

A recent study of U.S. business training and development practices reveals that the average U.S. company spends about one-half of one percent of its annual budget on employee training. This translates into approximately one and one-half days of training per person each year. In contrast, excellent companies invest about ten to fifteen work days per employee each year, or as much as ten times the average, on training.

It's no wonder that W. Edwards Deming put such a high premium on training. Two of his Fourteen Points of total quality deal with the subject. Quality begins, but never ends, with training. To remain qualified, people must continually update their knowledge and job skills. Every employee should be trained to recognize when a work process is in control and when it drifts out of control. Deming believed that by consistently training employees, variation in the output of their work would be reduced in much the same way that variation in a process is reduced through process controls.

In some organizations, employees are trained as generalists rather than specialists. Both employees and managers are expected to gain valuable experience in many areas of the company by moving from job to job. Management views such employees as well educated and able to handle material such as statistical concepts for quality control.

Education and training efforts point everyone in the organization toward one goal: producing the best possible products and services to satisfy the customer and then finding ways to make them better. Education and training are investments, not expenses, because they equip people to make solid business improvement decisions based on incisive analysis of data.

There are nine elements for the council to consider in sponsoring teams and providing resources.

Determine specific outcomes and team deliverables—There is an old saying that goes, "Tell them what you're going to tell them; tell them; and tell them what you think you told them." The point is to tell employees what you expect in terms of specific outcomes. Just what do you expect them to deliver? If there are no perceived deliverables, then tell them that as well.

Provide resources and remove barriers—Of all the resources that management is called upon to provide, the most crucial to success is training. Teaching employees how to master the key process skills—the interpersonal, the rational, and the implementing skills—should be a top priority for the council. About $1000 per employee is the universal average for annual training costs. Training needs to be timely and useful so that what is learned is soon put into practice.

Provide adequate time for teams to meet—The rule of thumb seems to be about two hours or so per person per week for actual team meetings. This does not count the additional time needed for individual assignments between meetings. Each meeting should have a formal agenda, and it is a good idea to have a recorder. Meeting space that is convenient and comfortable needs to be made available. (See *Team Building: A Structured Learning Approach* by Mears and Voehl.)

Provide team facilitation—There are two sources of team facilitation: internal and external facilitators. Whenever possible, internal facilitators should be used. This will help build the confidence and commitment needed for long-term continuity and growth. External facilitators can be useful in certain situations, such as when their particular background and objectivity are needed or when internal facilitators are not available. Facilitators can also be useful in supporting quality council meetings.

Instruct teams on regular reporting—The council should make clear to the teams when, why, and how to report progress. Generally, once a month is sufficient, unless unusual conditions call for more or less frequency. Reports from teams call for five fundamental areas to be covered, in a few paragraphs, concerning the results the teams have achieved and the strategy and process used:

- **Strong points**—What is going well?
- **Weak points**—What needs to be improved, eliminated, or replaced?
- **Learning points**—What did the team learn during the past month or quarter?
- **What are the expected outcomes and results to date?**
- **What are the next steps and expected completion date(s)?**

Engage employees in teams—Get employees involved in meaningful projects and team activities. As with any engagement, there is a period of courtship and pursuit, followed by embracement. The employees are only going to embrace the quality philosophy up to a certain point and only if management is willing to make the process interesting and stimulating. The "Five-i" process for employee engagement developed by Philip R. Thomas is a useful guideline:

- **Inspiration**—Planting the seed to improve or create
- **Identification**—People have to know how much they can improve
- **Information**—Data and training on how to collect and use data

- **Implementation**—Problem solving and carrying through to installation
- **Institutionalization**—A big word for locking in improvement with appropriate measures and controls

Provide for employee input opportunities—The council should provide opportunities for employee input, both formally and informally. Input can be obtained by allocating time on the council meeting agenda for team input and presentations; through visits to team work areas; through notes, letters, and memos; through e-mail and electronic bulletin boards; through point-of-service and other surveys; and so on. The key here is to be sure that feedback channels are designed into the process and then to act on feedback once received.

Coordinate activities—The process of coordinating and channeling activities has a direct impact on the effectiveness of team activities. Just as two teams should not be working on the same problem, so should all efforts be in harmony, with the right things taking place at the right time and in the right sequence. Because coordination is very time consuming, various tasks are usually "sponsored out" to individual members. Of all the project management/coordination tools available, the Program Evaluation and Reporting Technique (PERT) chart has proven to be one of the most useful.

Solicit feedback—This is something that needs to be done proactively instead of waiting for news to come to you. Council members need to actively solicit feedback from three sources:

- **The work/process**
- **Supervisors and employees**
- **Customers, both external and internal (clients)**

Feedback surveys, such as point-of-service, may be useful in evaluating the level of service provided by internal support departments in order to evaluate the following areas of satisfaction: accuracy, responsiveness, and timeliness (ART).

Exercise 11

Sponsoring Teams and Providing Resources

Instructions:

Get together in your assigned team and appoint a team leader. Spend fifteen minutes identifying the elements of your strategy for sponsoring teams and providing team resources.

Then privately take ten minutes to write down the key factors that should be reported on in that area. Record your ideas on Worksheet 11. Be prepared to explain why you feel that what you have identified is a key (i.e., critical) factor.

Then get back together as a team. Your team has thirty minutes to try to reach consensus on the major strategies and factors for each initiative. Limit your reporting requirements to a couple (three or four maximum) of factors. Your team leader will then explain the ideas to the larger group.

Worksheet 11

Strategies for Sponsoring Teams and Providing Resources	
Support Systems for Teams	
Areas of Focus	Specific Actions and Associated Indicators

Coaching and Communicating

> If I had a brick for every time I've repeated the phrase "Quality, Service, Cleanliness, and Value," I think I'd probably be able to bridge the Atlantic Ocean with them.
>
> *Ray Kroc*
> Founder of McDonald's

On the Art of Listening Down (from *Quality in Action*)

The most neglected aspect of corporate communication is "listening down." Few executives would maintain that they have nothing to learn from the people who buy their products and services. Yet these same executives act as if their employees have little of value to say. They treat internal communication solely as a way to make their views known, rarely actively soliciting opinions from those lower on the corporate ladder—unless they require a specific piece of information to make a specific decision.

The reason for this shortsighted behavior is an inability to acknowledge that, unlike corporate power, knowledge is not hierarchical. While it is proper to assume that the boss has the power to direct subordinates to perform some task, knowledge does not work in the same neat way.

If people believe that knowledge is hierarchical, it chokes off communication up the corporate ladder. If, for instance, someone sees a problem that is causing some loss in efficiency, he or she might think, "Well, I can see that there's a problem here...so my boss must see it too, since it is so obvious to me. But my boss doesn't direct it to be fixed...so my boss must know something else that I don't know which makes it necessary to do it this seemingly inefficient way. So I guess I'll just keep doing it this way as well as I can."

In truth, of course, the boss has not seen the particular inefficiency, and if alerted to it would know of no reason to continue it.

Listening down comes with assumptions and guidelines of its own:

- Not all wisdom is above you on the corporate ladder. Listening up only gives part of the picture.
- Listening down leads to decision making that is far better informed. There is no cause for shame in not knowing it all; there is a cause for shame in refusing to listen.
- Whether at the top of the organization or at the bottom, it is impossible to make intelligent decisions without accurate information. Withholding information is self-defeating.
- Successful listening includes taking action as a result of what is learned.
- Form can precede content. Formalized rules (e.g., a resolution to talk with three non-management employees every Monday afternoon) are excellent ways to start new habits. (*Quality in Action*)

Important Elements in Coaching and Communicating

1. Communicate the vision, direction, and current situation—Exemplary organizations often have a five-year road map for each department which shows a clear vision of how the organization expects to become and remain best-in-class. Reviews of progress on these road maps are held regularly. Also, road maps are consistent and complementary across functional boundaries. Road maps are often shared with key customers. Everyone in the department is aware of the key development strategies/plans and their respective roles.

2. Implement a personal coaching plan—Every member of the council should have his or her own personal coaching plan involving every employee in the department. The objective is to reach each employee in order to give everyone a chance to make their own unique contribution to winning and develop the self-confidence that winning brings.

3. Post measures in all organization work areas—Measures for key indicators that track progress on at least a monthly basis should be posted in all work areas. The display should be in the form of graphs and charts, where possible.

4. Keep everyone informed.

5. Communicate team results and council decisions—Communication (the art of keeping everyone informed) is the mortar that binds the quality journey together. As top management's vision of quality gets filtered down through the ranks, the vision and the quality message can lead to misunderstanding and loss of momentum. Management guru Peter Drucker concludes, "The communications gap within institutions and between groups in society has been widening steadily, to a point where it threatens to become an unbridgeable gulf of total misunderstanding." Notwithstanding this gulf of misunderstanding, Drucker's theory of "managerial communications" in organizations may provide help in the quality management process. To paraphrase the essence of his principles:

- One can only communicate in terms of the recipient's language and perception and, therefore, the message must be in terms of the recipient's own experience. If the employee's perception of quality is "do a better job" or "keep the customer happy," the message of total quality management is unlikely to be understood. *Suggestion:* Measures of quality should be set and agreed upon.
- Only the recipient can communicate; the communicator cannot. Thus, management systems, including training, should be designed from the point of view of the recipient and with feedback built in. *Suggestion:* Feedback and thus the exchange of information should be based on some measure, target, benchmark, or standard that the employee (recipient) is involved in setting. All information is coded, and there must be prior agreement on the meaning of the code. Make sure that quality is carefully defined and measures agreed upon.

- Communication "downward" cannot work because it focuses on what we want to say. *Suggestion:* Communicate upward by encouraging employees to set measurable goals and then converting them into action plans. (Listen downward to become better informed.)

6. Share key feedback—As previously mentioned, sharing brings everyone into the loop. When employees are involved in developing the feedback mechanism, acceptance is high. The formula for effectiveness is

Effectiveness = Quality × Acceptance × Feedback

When feedback is low, effectiveness is reduced. When feedback is missing, effectiveness equals zero.

Exercise 12

Coaching and Communicating

Instructions:

Get together in your assigned team and appoint a team leader. Spend ten minutes identifying the elements in the coaching and communicating practices area that your team will focus on. Then take ten minutes to individually identify the key factors that should be reported on in that area. Record your ideas on Worksheet 12. Be prepared to explain why you feel that what you have identified is a key (i.e., critical) factor.

Then get back together as a team. Your team has thirty minutes to try to reach consensus on the initiatives and factors to focus on. Limit your reporting requirements to a couple (three or four maximum) so that they will not become burdensome.

Your team leader will then explain the ideas your team came up with to the larger group.

Worksheet 12

Strategies for Coaching and Communicating	
Support Systems for Coaching and Communicating	
Areas of Focus	Specific Actions and Associated Indicators

Employee Involvement

Employee involvement can be encouraged through a series of exercises to help get employees to buy into the idea of quality improvement. Exercises 13 and 14 are provided as examples to give you a feeling for what employees will be experiencing. Unless you are personally willing to understand what is being asked of your employees, then you cannot expect them to seriously embrace the concept of quality improvement.

Second, ideas will be developed for recognition programs to reinforce employee involvement. Third, we will discuss the concept of reporting quality results, and, finally, performance reviews will be discussed.

CQI requires the full commitment of both management and employees. Even if management is committed, the process is doomed to fail unless employees are actively involved in and committed to the task of improving the quality of the goods and services they provide.

Ideas will be presented throughout this workbook to increase employee involvement in the quality improvement process. During CQI training, participants will be asked to assist in defining quality in their jobs by identifying indicators of high quality in their jobs (see Exercise 13).

It is often difficult to begin the process of quality improvement because there are so many aspects to a particular problem. Quality ideas may be so large and external that tackling them would likely be unproductive. On the other hand, some ideas my be small internal ideas that are within our control (see Exercise 14).

Remember, unless you are willing to take these exercise seriously, and "personalize" the process of quality improvement, you cannot expect your employees to become committed to quality improvement.

Exercise 13

Quality Indicators

Instructions:

Break into teams and select a team leader who will lead the discussion to identify subjective quality measures. Take ten minutes to privately complete Worksheet 13. We are not concerned with physical aspects (such as speed, performance, reliability), but instead are concerned with a more personal perspective.

Think about a service you received that you liked. Why did you like it? The reason you liked it is often a subjective attribute and may be attributed to accompanying events, such as the service received in a restaurant with pleasant surroundings from someone with a nice personality who went that "extra step" to give you good service.

Identify four quality indicators either in your job or in a job similar to yours. Record your ideas on Worksheet 13. Then share your thoughts on indicators of high quality with your team members.

Worksheet 13

Quality Indicators

Indicators of High Quality	
Product or Service Received	**Quality Indicator**

Exercise 14

Tackling Quality Problems

Instructions:

Break into teams and select a team leader who will lead the discussion to identify quality problems or opportunities for teams to work on. Take ten minutes to privately complete Worksheet 14. Identify quality improvement ideas for areas that you deal with in your organization. Record your ideas on the worksheet. Can you think of any improvement ideas using the worksheets in previous exercises? Feel free to go back and change any worksheet if a new idea occurs to you.

After identifying quality improvement ideas in each category, rank the difficulty of correcting the problem from 1 (easy to accomplish) to 7 (difficult to accomplish). Then get together with your team and share your thoughts with others.

Worksheet 14

Tackling Quality Problems

Ranking Quality Improvement Ideas

Idea		Rank
Small Internal Ideas:	__________	____
	__________	____
	__________	____
Small External Ideas:	__________	____
	__________	____
	__________	____
Large Internal Ideas:	__________	____
	__________	____
	__________	____
Large External Ideas:	__________	____
	__________	____
	__________	____

Ranking: 1 = easiest to accomplish, 7 = most difficult to accomplish

Personal Quality Checklist

Who has responsibility for installing CQI? Is it solely the organization's responsibility, or does the employee share some of the responsibility for implementing CQI? If you take the broad view that CQI is a philosophy which involves continuous improvement on the behalf of everyone (society, the community, the organization, and the employee), then everyone should share the responsibility for installing CQI in their organization and in their personal lives.

A personal quality checklist is an excellent way to demonstrate management commitment and to get employees personally involved in CQI by showing the way. The checklist encourages council members to keep track of personal items (defects). The mere act of itemizing the personal defects that you want to improve upon is a step toward showing your commitment to improvement. Keeping track of the defects serves as a reminder to pay attention to those important items, and improvement tends to "automatically" follow.

The hardest part of developing a personal quality checklist is identifying the items that should be on the checklist. We'll share a personal checklist with you here as an example. Remember, however, this is not your checklist; it is one of the authors', and your items will undoubtedly differ.

Personal Quality Checklist: Peter Mears								
Week of:								
Defect Category	**Sun**	**Mon**	**Tues**	**Wed**	**Thurs**	**Fri**	**Sat**	**Total**
Excessive handling of paperwork								
Delayed return of forms								
Not prepared for meetings								
Office not clean at end of day								
Not answering phone within two rings								
Typos in correspondence								

Peter Mears is a university professor, and teaching is the "fun" part of his job. The "hard" part is that, in addition to research, a lot of coordination with students and higher administration is required. Mr. Mears handles an immense amount of paperwork. Therefore, his primary improvement item is to stop the excessive handling of paperwork. What often occurs is that instead of immediately answering a message left in his mailbox, he thinks about it and places the message in his attaché case. Then he carries the message around and looks at it a couple of times. After a number of weeks pass, the messages stack up, and he is "forced" to finally answer them.

Undoubtedly, some messages require a lot of thought, but most messages in his teaching job are simple requests that can be handled immediately. Mr. Mears is making a mountain out of a mole hill, as the saying goes, by his excessive handling of his messages. Hence, every time he handles the same request, he will count it as an error.

Some complex messages will indeed require double handling, but they are very few in number. Of course, this means that he will never get to zero messages, but he has never thought of himself as a zero defects person. However, the goal is to become a more efficient person.

The second checklist category, "delayed return of forms" (including official correspondence), is related to the first category, but again, Mr. Mears' checklist is concerned with personal improvement items. Many forms and official correspondence require that a statistic be referenced before responding (a grade, a student no longer in class, a meeting time, request for information, etc.), which, of course, means that the correspondence will have to be handled several times. This category is not included in the first tally, and the goal here is to answer all such correspondence within one working day. This goal may be unreasonable, because some correspondence requires input from other people, who may not respond quickly to Mr. Mears' request. However, needing a simple working definition of what is or is not acceptable, he is going to leave the goal at one day for the time being.

Another personal improvement item involves the habit of not answering phone calls quickly. There is a reason for this. When the phone rings, he is either talking to someone who is in the office or is busy trying to complete what he is doing before answering the phone. But why wait? His thought process has effectively been destroyed by the ringing phone, and since he is going to have to answer the phone sooner or later anyway, he is going to try answering it within two rings.

The category "office not clean at end of day" is the result of poor work habits. At the end of a day, he simply stops what he is doing and leaves, leaving everything in a mess or partially completed. That must stop! The goal is to complete everything and deliver it (i.e., no out-basket, take it to the mail room on the way out). If something absolutely cannot be completed, it will be placed in an in-basket. Thus, there will be no half-completed work and no stack of paper on his desk to face in the morning. If there is, it will be recorded as an error.

Although each department has secretaries, they are often monopolized by administrators, and professors usually have to type their own correspondence. Mr. Mears has learned how to type, but has not learned how to spell. Embarrassed by his typos, he has purchased a pocket dictionary and will use it if in doubt about any spelling. Recording these errors will be difficult, because if an error can be detected, it will be corrected immediately; hence it is not an error because it has been corrected. We are sure psychologists could have a "field day" with this type of logic, but this is Mr. Mears' checklist, and he is determined to keep track of errors as something that he did wrong, after the item left his control.

Did the personal quality checklist work?—We don't know if the personal quality checklist modified Mr. Mears' behavior. However, he feels more in control of most items. Frankly, however, some days his phone rings so many times (particularly on Monday mornings) and he records so many defects that he simply gives up. In any event, Mr. Mears has revised his checklist to temporarily remove that item until he can figure out how to better organize those "high-volume" days. However, he knows that he is working smarter in handling paperwork and is forcing himself to respond more quickly, particularly to routine forms and correspondence.

Where will it all end? Will Mr. Mears ever construct a good personal quality checklist that he can live with? We tend to doubt it, because continuous quality improvement is a never-ending process.

If you want your employees to buy into a quality improvement effort, then start keeping your own personal quality improvement checklist. You don't have to make a big deal out of it. After a few weeks, people will pick up on what you are doing.

For additional information on personal checklists, see "Using Personal Checklists to Facilitate TQM" by Harry V. Roberts (*Quality Progress,* June 1993, pp. 51–56).

Exercise 15

Your Own Quality Improvement Checklist

Instructions:

Use the form provided in Worksheet 15 as a guide to construct your own personal quality improvement checklist. If you are not going to create your own checklist—and take it seriously—how can you expect your employees to buy into the concept of continuous quality improvement?

Worksheet 15

Personal Quality Checklist

Personal Quality Checklist:

Week of:

Defect Category	Sun	Mon	Tues	Wed	Thurs	Fri	Sat	Total

Recognition and Rewards

I can live two months on a good compliment.
Mark Twain

The category—recognition—is a more controversial investment. The essential focus of such a program is to say thank you, thank you to all deserving people in ways both symbolic and material. But, as with every other aspect of expenditure in a quality process, it is a proven investment.
Pat Townsend

Webster's New Collegiate Dictionary defines recognition as a "special notice or attention." A survey of Baldrige finalists identifies the recognition system as a uniform method for management to demonstrate their appreciation to quality improvement participants for their efforts toward achieving quality objectives. The survey shows that quality improvement participants may be recognized for their:

- **Voluntary membership in the quality program with a membership pin**
- **Participation in solving their first improvement opportunity with a tangible promotional item (a visible means of showing completion of an improvement action)**
- **Implementation of each improvement action thereafter by managerial acknowledgment**
- **Achievement as top performers through semi-annual luncheons hosted by local managers and a semi-annual dinner with spouses on a quality council and corporate level.**

Organizations such as Domino's Pizza, North American Tool & Die, AT&T, Xerox, Motorola, and others recognize achievement with parties, awards, celebrations, and plenty of public pats on the back. Every manager and supervisor should be expected to recognize successes and accomplishments, large and small. The rewards do not have to be formal or bureaucratic; they can be spontaneous and personal, appropriate to the circumstance. Excellent organizations also include "having fun at work" as a goal when setting performance objectives. They ask their employees what they think is fun and then try to fit the fun to each person and each situation.

Each quality council is responsible for administering a recognition program in a fashion consistent with its vision and values. There are six core support elements to be addressed by the council when implementing recognition programs.

1. Determine appropriate recognition systems and items—The right types of behaviors must be reinforced by a reward and recognition program that conveys items of tangible value and other forms of personal satisfaction to those individuals and groups practicing them. Not only will this reinforce the new behaviors, but it will also send a powerful message about values, beliefs, and what actions merit rewards. There are various types of cash and non-cash recognition items that can be used by the council, including bonuses, equity arrangements, gifts, gainsharing, and other monetary incentives. Non-cash items range from pens, to windbreakers or sweatshirts, to dinners, shows, parties, etc. Recognition includes verbal and written praise. It may also include symbolic items, such as certificates, plaques, and jewelry. Studies have shown that recognition motivation schemes tend to last longer than financial rewards and are very effective in reinforcing behaviors to produce desirable outcomes.[1] The system and items should be tailored to the nature and personality of the department or organization.

2. Integrate contributions to business objectives into performance appraisal—Each individual should be given the opportunity to have his or her contribution to the business objectives reflected in the performance appraisal. In this way, the performance appraisal becomes part of the recognition process instead of a negative experience. There should be prior agreement as to the items to be tracked and included. Personal and professional growth must be important elements that are designed into the system.

3. Hold local recognition ceremonies and dinners—One of the most important forms of recognition is at the local level, where individuals and teams are recognized in front of their peers. A dinner with spouses present is also a useful form. Luncheons and dinners should be budgeted for by local management.

4. Sponsor teams to present before the quality council—Team reward and recognition has become a major component of any CQI system. Research shows that most companies that exhibit world-class quality practices invest heavily in major company-wide group celebration activities.[2] The teams should be coached in the manner of presenting data in the most concise manner possible. All team members should be encouraged to attend the presentation, although it is not necessary for all of them to have a part. The local quality council should then provide feedback to the team.

Monday Morning Mirror Issues

Recognition can be tricky. What simple technique can I use?

Catch your employees doing something right, and thank them.

5. Reward employees for team and individual contributions—As previously mentioned, the rewards should be a combination of cash and non-cash types, especially where individual or team contributions are reflected in a person's performance appraisal. Communication and understanding of the exact criteria are important to support an effective system. Employees need to know what exact behaviors will result in recognition and/or reward.

6. Publish results—Measuring the success of a reward and recognition program must be tied directly to the achievement and success of the organization's strategic objectives. Various methods of publishing results should be used, including television, videos, newsletters, memos, director and manager group meetings, etc. The important thing is to let the teams and individuals see that their results are worth talking about. According to an old truism, "Effectiveness is measured by results."

The following are a few final thoughts to consider when creating a recognition program to support a CQI system:[3]

- The program must be enthusiastically supported by top management.
- The program should not be tied to compensation for doing the job. Compensation is a right; recognition is a gift.
- An organization-wide committee of upbeat managers and award winners should administer the program. Rotate membership on the committee for fresh ideas.
- Candidates are recommended to the committee in writing by supervisors. Specific accomplishments should be documented.

- Teams as well as individuals are recognized.
- The time lag between submission of nominations and award presentations should be less than three weeks. A time delay weakens the impact of awards given for special accomplishments.
- Deliver awards in a personal manner. Avoid grand productions. Try lunch with the CEO or pictures in the newsletter.
- Be on the lookout for employees to nominate. Catch people doing something right.
- Widely publicize winners and why they won. Identify what management considers a heroic effort.
- Give awards that employees value (tickets to major events, the CEO's parking space for a month, dinner for two at a local restaurant).

The issue of monetary awards for quality improvements is tricky and can easily fill an academic textbook. The standard rule in such programs is to keep it simple. The most effective award structure is to provide quick, positive feedback to the action you want to reinforce as soon as possible.

Exercise caution in giving awards whenever something positive is performed, because in CQI, people are constantly supposed to make that "extra effort" to improve service quality. However, for either outstanding individual effort or effort on behalf of a team, treating individuals or groups to dinner for two at a local restaurant is a gentle way for an organization to say "thanks." It is further reinforced when each person dines with a guest of his or her choice.

Endnotes

1. In the July 1994 issue of *Quality Digest,* a report entitled "Reward and Recognition" by Ron Cassell highlights how motivating employees plays a key role in creating a continuous improvement culture. According to the author, those organizations that are able to successfully make this change will be addressing the one component left out of many continuous improvement efforts—the human condition.
2. Source: Ron Cassell, *Quality Digest,* July 1994, p. 54.
3. See Sam Deep and Lyle Sussman, *The Manager's Book of Lists,* University of Louisville, School of Business, 1988.

Exercise 16

Developing a Recognition and Reward Program

Instructions:

Take ten minutes to individually identify ideas for a recognition and reward program that would be effective in your organization. Record your ideas on Worksheet 16. Then get back together as a team. Your team has twenty minutes to try to reach consensus on the five major ideas that could be incorporated in an employee recognition and reward program in your organization. Your team leader will then explain these ideas to the larger group.

Worksheet 16

Developing a Recognition and Reward Program

Ideas for a recognition and reward program to reinforce quality improvement:

Chapter 7

Reporting and Evaluating Quality Results

Quality, like beauty, is an elusive concept and is in the eyes of the beholder. But that doesn't mean that we have to ignore it. It just means that we have to try harder to quantify the important aspects of quality as seen from the perspective of our customers. Once measurements are in place, they can be monitored to determine if improvements are occurring.

The issue of quantifying the factors that make up quality is extremely important. Suppose someone were to say, "We have improved our customer satisfaction." Would you really believe them? If so, which customers are more satisfied with what variables? In short, if you can't measure it, you can't improve it.

Before the detailed processes that lead to quality goods and services can be quantified, those process must be thoroughly understood. Quality factors for measurement by management will be discussed in greater detail in the section on the Baldrige Award in Chapter 13.

Monday Morning Mirror Issues

Increased information to employees decreases rumors.

Decreased information increases rumors.

When initially installing a continuous quality improvement system, encourage employee involvement by asking employees to report quality results. Be rather flexible and accept either hard data results or indicators of quality results. Hard data results are based on facts, including surveys. Indicators of quality results are factors such as employee suggestions for improvement, attendance at quality improvement seminars, participation on task teams, consumer surveys, etc. (This topic is also discussed in the next chapter on group empowerment.)

Monday Morning Mirror Issues

OK! So, I'll send everyone to a quality training program, and that's the end of the problem!

A program can't change attitudes that have developed over a lifetime.

Exercise 17

Reporting Key Quality Factors

Instructions:

Get together in your assigned team and appoint a team leader. Take ten minutes to identify the department (or area) in your organization that your team will focus on. Then take ten minutes to individually identify the key quality factors that should be reported on in that area. Use Worksheet 17 to record your ideas. Be prepared to explain why you feel what you have identified is a key (i.e., critical) quality factor.

Then get back together as a team. Your team has thirty minutes to try to reach consensus on the major quality factors for that department or area. Limit your reporting requirements to a couple (three maximum) of factors so that the reporting requirements will not become burdensome.

Your team leader will then explain the department and the quality reporting ideas to the larger group.

Worksheet 17

Key Quality Factors

Key Quality Factors for Department
Key (critical) factors:
Why are these factors critical? (Be specific)

Performance Evaluations: Overview

A continuous quality improvement system needs reinforcement to be successful. To borrow from the thinking of Juran, a powerful way to reinforce the importance of quality in an organization is to incorporate critical quality indicators into managerial and employee performance evaluations. However, employees and most supervisors consider performance evaluations the most distasteful part of their jobs. Therefore, it may not be easy to get employees to suggest performance indicators when they know they will be evaluated on making improvements in these areas. Although this problem cannot completely be resolved, a few suggestions are in order.

The major purposes of performance appraisals are:

To Evaluate:

- **To make a compensation decision**
- **To make a promotion decision**
- **To make a discipline or discharge decision**

To Develop:

- **To communicate performance expectations**
- **To identify areas in need of improvement**
- **To identify programs and activities that will enable the employee to grow and develop**

Performance evaluations should be based on job-related behaviors and results expected and not on personality traits. Avoid evaluations based on personal characteristics such as loyalty, cooperation, work habits, and dependability. These characteristics tend to be too general.

A **critical incident technique** can be used to establish performance requirements. This is accomplished by conducting a departmental meeting with the stated purpose of identifying quality performance goals. Stress that the objective of the meeting is to develop goals that reflect a high level of service. Furthermore, meaningful goals will be included in the annual performance review process.

If employees do not offer quality goals, share with them improvement ideas you are considering and ask for suggestions. In addition, ask them what they can do during the year to improve the quality of their services (i.e., another way of asking for improvement goals).

Evaluating Customer Service Personnel

Customer service representatives (CSRs) include bank tellers, airline ticket sellers, car rental agents, and numerous others whose jobs involve interacting with the public. The behavior demonstrated by CSRs strongly influences customer satisfaction regarding services. CSRs can build customer relations through a high level of service and a personalized concern.

CSR personnel should recognize customers as individuals and make the customer's life more pleasant by resolving his or her problem. The customer should be made to feel comfortable and important.

CSRs should present themselves professionally and convey an excitement about their work. They should have confidence in themselves and their co-workers so that they deliver the best services possible.

Performance-Based CSR Evaluation

SPECIFIC FACTORS:	Strongly Disagree				Strongly Agree	Not Observed
1. Greets customer before customer greets him or her.	1	2	3	4	5	0
2. Greets customers with a smile.	1	2	3	4	5	0
3. Makes eye contact.	1	2	3	4	5	0
4. Anticipates customers' problems and provides whatever necessary to make customers comfortable.	1	2	3	4	5	0
5. Asks customers what they need.	1	2	3	4	5	0
6. Checks with customers to determine if service was satisfactory.	1	2	3	4	5	0
7. Follows up on customer problems.	1	2	3	4	5	0
8. Uses customer's name with Mr., Mrs., or Ms. when addressing him or her	1	2	3	4	5	0
APPEARANCE/ATTITUDE:	**Strongly Disagree**				**Strongly Agree**	**Not Observed**
9. Appearance is neat, clean, and tidy.	1	2	3	4	5	0
10. Keeps composure even when customers are irate.	1	2	3	4	5	0
11. Communicates positive feedback to co-workers.	1	2	3	4	5	0
12. Reflects a positive attitude.	1	2	3	4	5	0

Describe your observations of the CSR you are evaluating. Describe what you have observed the employee doing during the performance period. Use words such as enters, smiles, inserts, orders, greets, friendly, etc. to describe CSR actions.

Overall description of what you observed:

CSR's Name/Identifier: ______________________________

Observer: ______________________________

Date Observed: ______________________________

Adapted from R.W. Beatty, "Competitive Human Resource Advantage through Strategic Management of Performance." *Human Resource Planning,* 1989, No. 3, pp. 185–186.

Exercise 18

Task-Based Performance Evaluations

Instructions:

Get together in your assigned team and appoint a team leader. The leader's job is to assist the group in selecting a customer service representative in your organization for analysis. Take ten minutes to individually identify five major quality factors that should be incorporated in the evaluation. Record your ideas on Worksheet 18. Indicate how each quality factor will be identified in the evaluation in a manner so that results can be reported back to the employee.

Then get back together as a team. Your team has thirty minutes to try to reach consensus on important customer interaction factors that should be included in the employee's evaluation.

Your team leader will then explain these ideas to the larger group.

Worksheet 18

Customer Service Representative: ______________________________

Performance evaluation factors:

Employee Performance Evaluations

Indicators of quality should be considered in some manner in performance reviews for both management and, later, for employees. These indicators may be relatively general and can consist of factors such as number of ideas submitted, working on quality improvement teams, and the like. However, sooner or later, organizations should consider Juran's approach to sustaining a continuous quality improvement program. Specific quality improvement goals should be set, plans should be established to meet those goals, and progress should be measured. Progress toward meeting quality improvement goals should be evaluated and incorporated into a formal annual performance review process.

Monday Morning Mirror Issues

Dr. Deming was right when he said -

"People who expect quick results are doomed to disappointment."

Exercise 19

Employee Performance Evaluations

Instructions:

Get together in your assigned team and appoint a team leader. The leader's job is to assist the group in selecting a category of salaried employees for evaluation. Using Worksheet 19, each team member is to spend ten minutes writing his or her ideas about what quality factors should be included in the employee's performance evaluation.

Then meet as a team and try to reach consensus on the three or four major factors that should be included in the evaluation. Identify any stumbling blocks that will have to be overcome in order for this change to be implemented. Your team leader will then explain these ideas to the larger group.

Worksheet 19

Quality Factors for Incorporation in Performance Evaluations

Employee category:

Quality factors:

Rethinking Executive Performance Evaluations

Let's face it—it is easier to say you are committed to a quality improvement process than it is to take positive steps that lead the organization forward. Dr. Juran is very frank on this point:

> Quality improvements are necessary if the organization is to survive. Therefore, quality improvements should be formally controlled, and progress against those goals should be monitored and evaluated.

Traditional financial accounting measures like return on investment and earnings per share can give misleading signals to executives in organizations seeking continuous improvement and innovation—activities that today's competitive marketplace demands. The remedy is a balanced scorecard approach for senior executives, first developed by Kaplan and Norton in 1992.

Robert Kaplan and David Nolan first developed the new look at executive measures as a result of their work which was first published in the *Harvard Business Review* ("The Balanced Scorecard—Measures that Drive Performance." January–February 1992, pp. 71–79). This work was expanded into many corporate boardrooms and resulted in sweeping changes in the way executive compensation is calculated. These changes have been well documented in the quality journeys of Florida Power and Light and Xerox.

This approach is represented by a group or family of measures that summarize progress toward the objectives most important to the organization. The approach was validated through a year-long study with twelve companies to explore ways of finding the combination of operational and financial measures that would constitute a "balanced scorecard." The conclusion was that there are four important measurement perspectives for performance review of executives:

- **Financial perspective: How do we look to our shareholders?**
- **Customer perspective: How do customers see us?**
- **Internal business perspective: What must we excel at?**
- **Innovation and learning perspective: Can we continue to create value?**

Each of these perspectives implies a set of goals, which in turn imply certain measures of performance in achieving and exceeding those goals. Finally, each executive must create an individual balanced scorecard for his or her unique circumstances.

Exercise 20

Executive Performance Evaluations

Instructions:

Get together in your assigned team and appoint a team leader. Take fifteen minutes to identify ideas for an executive performance evaluation program that will be effective in your organization. Identify any stumbling blocks that will have to be overcome in order for this change to be effective. Record your ideas on Worksheet 20.

Then get back together as a team. Your team has thirty minutes to try to reach consensus on five or six major ideas that could be incorporated in an executive performance evaluation in your organization. Your team leader will then explain these ideas to the larger group.

Worksheet 20

Executive Performance Evaluation

Executive Performance Evaluation:

Balanced Scorecard of Performance Factors

Financial factors:

Customer-related factors:

Chapter 8

Empowerment, Engagement, and Encouragement

Empowerment: An organizational state where people are aligned with the business direction and understand their performance boundaries, thus enabling them to take responsibility and ownership while seeking improvements, identifying the best course of action and initiating steps to satisfy customer requirements.

Xerox Corporate Management Institute

Putting Empowerment to Work

The concept of empowerment, when coupled with engagement and encouragement, is fundamental to continuous quality improvement. Everyone in the organization should be empowered to continuously improving their work processes in order to yield higher degrees of customer satisfaction. In a recent study, the case for empowerment was made as follows: "A leader's job is one of building humane communities where people can pour their hearts and minds into significant work that builds a better world."[1] In other words, leaders need to master the "human process" expertise, which requires a new psychological contract between manager and employee. The bottom line is that senior management must own the empowerment initiative; it cannot be delegated. According to an old axiom, "It is part of our nature to measure ourselves by our intentions and others by their behavior." This is at the heart of what we call "the empowerment dilemma." All leaders want an empowered work force, yet few are aware of how their own behavior gets in the way. This often sends a false signal to employees that management is more interested in control, personal power, politics, status, and recognition than in true empowerment of the employees. The issues that will be dealt with in this chapter can help avoid these pitfalls.

The heart of empowerment is people on teams—In a smoothly functioning quality improvement system, teams of empowered employees operate relatively autonomously. It might sound simple to have groups engaged in autonomous operations, but it isn't. Group members must function together as a team. However, do not assume that simply by calling a group of employees a "team" they will automatically function as a team and the organization will reap the benefits. In reality, it just doesn't happen that way. Groups must go through a change process to begin functioning as a team. Training will be needed to develop self-awareness and decision-making ability. In addition, assistance will be needed in establishing a mission (direction) for the team.

The soul of empowerment is power—Information is power in the organization of the future. This often leads to an overproduction of data by employees who may want to create an aura of indispensability, which often leads to information overload. Under conditions in which information is organized for ease of use by employees, the empowerment process and all its benefits should thrive.[2]

The mind of empowerment is continuous improvement—This type of thinking has its roots in pride and achievement. A recent study[3] of empowered organizations by William Byham identified fourteen key factors that are shared by empowered organizations. These factors, along with others, are incorporated into the following support structures for creating the empowered organization.

Monday Morning Mirror Issues

How can I install team building if my executives don't get along together?

You can't.

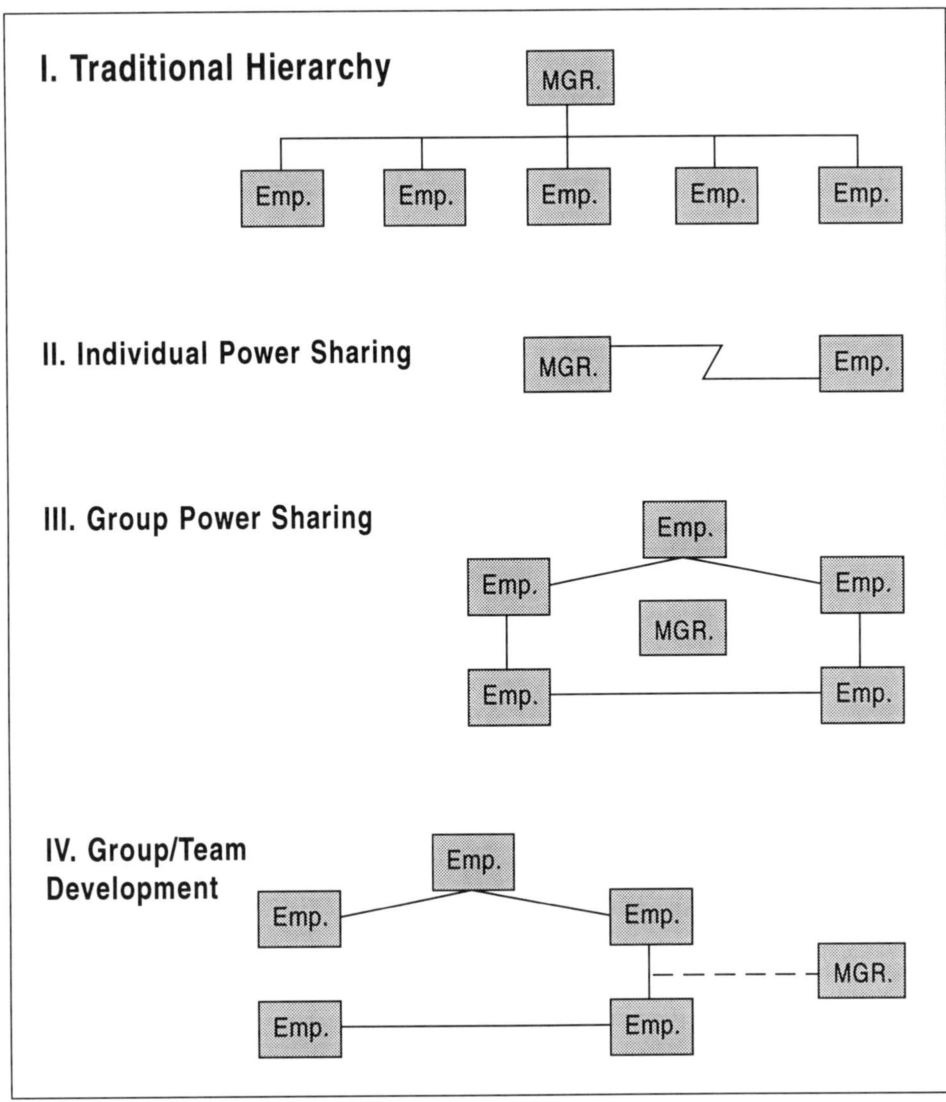

Team Development

Support Systems

The following support systems are useful to help make the initiative of empowering, engaging, and encouraging come alive.

Understand what empowerment is all about—Understanding the meaning of empowerment at each organizational level, as well as how to achieve it, is vital. The roles of empowerment work teams and support groups, as well as organizational systems (information systems, travel reimbursement policies, etc.) must be clearly thought through.

Discuss the vision and expectations in ways the employees can relate to and understand—The point of this initiative is to communicate the desired outcomes to all employees and ultimately secure their buy in. As previously mentioned, this can be done as early as during the interview and selection process. The vision and values should be prominently displayed. A three- to five-year time line of events is often helpful, both on a corporate and a departmental basis. Ask for feedback and have employees restate the desired outcomes in their own words. Use the vision and values to guide decision making.

Don't overpromise or understate—There is a tendency when trying to motivate employees to overcommit and paint a rosy picture, as well as to minimize the need for extra effort. Be honest with employees, and they will respect you. Also, design performance management systems that provide clear and honest understanding of job responsibilities and methods for measuring success.

Establish teams to fit the system—The quality council must form teams to focus on systemic problems, including job design teams to build in more ownership and accountability. Also, management must learn the problem-solving tools and techniques that can be used to get the job done, which often means participating on teams as well. This also includes giving guidance and direction on areas to work on and areas to avoid before any teams are formed. Once the overall strategy for system improvement has been determined, it is time to get the employees involved in the details of system improvement. Together, management and employees become a very powerful partnership in system improvement.

Engage employees to participate[4]—There are three major areas for employees to focus on in the empowerment mode:

- **Business Process Analysis (BPA) teams need to be formed to map out key processes and build process ownership.**
- **Quality Improvement Teams (QITs) need to be formed to identify and implement improvements.**
- **Benchmarking teams need to be formed to work on breakthrough opportunities.**

Each quality council needs to carefully think out its strategy and rationale for forming empowerment teams in relation to the needs and objectives of the department. Employees are well aware when management abdicates responsibility. Allocation of resources, communication, training, teamwork/cooperation, and definition of specifications are all management issues. Unless management is willing to solve these problems, employees cannot be expected to solve problems in their own work areas.

Encourage people to identify and bring forth problems—Employees who are encouraged to take risks to solve problems do so. Lack of initiative is often directly related to rules and regulations that limit alternatives. Let employees know when it is okay to go beyond the regulations and take some risks, and praise them for it. The goal should be to encourage employees to take calculated, plausible risks instead of punishing them for errors. Mistakes should be viewed as opportunities for learning.

In the 1986 Presidential Commission Report on the Challenger accident, the two main contributing causes of the accident were (1) the failure of a simple $10 "O-ring" and (2) a complex project management infrastructure which did not facilitate the upward flow of bad news. This failure on the part of NASA management to encourage people to bring forth problems had disastrous effects from which the organization still has not fully recovered. It is the job of the quality council to place a premium on employees bringing forth problems. Learn not to shoot the messenger. If the messenger gets shot, no one will want to play the role, and problems will remain hidden due to a lack of willing messengers. Praise the messengers—don't shoot them.

Provide data collection systems—Problems often lay buried or uncovered because of the lack of effective methods and systems for collecting data. This does not always mean computer systems. Many times, simple manual collection systems (such as check sheets and graphs) in the hands of the right people are enough. Also, the collection of information must be done in a discriminate way. Finding out "all there is to know" not only wastes time, effort, and money, but can actually impede the solution of a problem by burying the problem solvers under an avalanche of irrelevant, unmanageable detail. Therefore, the data collection system must assist in gathering information selectively.

Provide input and access to the quality council by empowerment teams—Input needs to be provided by the empowerment teams at key stages in the problem-solving process. Usually, this is done at four points:

- **When the issue or problem to be worked on is selected**
- **When the problem statement is defined**
- **When the solution/benefits are identified for implementation**
- **When the implementation plan has been developed**

Coordinate—One of the key aspects of coordination on the part of the quality council is to break down the barriers between departments. It is the quality council's job to ensure that representatives from customer and supplier groups are included in focus groups to provide information for problem solving. Coordination is needed if people are to work as a team. Unions must also be involved where appropriate.

Be involved in solutions and provide for personal choices—The quality council must be actively involved in seeing that solutions are properly implemented. Council members cannot be bystanders on the sideline who say "I told you so" when things go wrong. Empowerment is a state of mind as well as the result of organizational practices. Empowerment stems from both the policies supported by management and the personal choices made by group members. To feel empowered means the individual:

- **Takes responsibility for his or her situation**
- **Has a vision of something worthwhile (i.e., a purpose for the work he or she does)**
- **Makes a commitment to achieving that purpose**

Has something like the following ever happened to you?

This type of run-around is not the fault of the student advising department. Each department involved in the process (student advising, student records, registrar, finance, bookstore, public safety, and student affairs) looks at its small portion of the process and probably feels it is efficient. These departments are part of a bureaucracy which has developed over time and is focused inward on individual departmental concerns. They are not focused on the needs of the customers.

A team approach is required to evaluate this condition, cut through the red tape, and empower the student advising office to do its job: advise students with a minimum of hassle.

If the advisor is empowered, what about the people who work in the support departments (student records, registrar, finance, bookstore, public safety, student affairs)? Will they lose power? When power is shared, not everyone gains. It is inevitable that the organization realign itself to reflect changing priorities. Management of some departments will most likely lose power. There is a tendency to fight any loss of power and prestige. The power of a manager is mostly derived from the number of employees in the department. All things being equal, the higher the head count, the higher the power and pay of the managerial position.

Meaningful Quality

For quality to be a personal and an organizational value:

- **It must be chosen freely**
- **It must be chosen from alternatives**
- **It must be acted upon by the person and the organization**
- **It must help people achieve their potential and help the organization achieve its potential**
- **It must be publicly affirmed by the person and the organization**

Sure, empowered employees will have to change their method of doing business, but frequently the result of an empowered organization is that there is less need for middle management.

Exercise 21

Building an Empowerment Strategy

Instructions:

Take ten minutes to individually identify ideas (strategies) for improving the effectiveness of empowered teams in your organization. Record your strategies on Worksheet 21. Express your strategies in the form of objectives. Be sure to assess individual/team desire for empowerment and the support structure that will assist the team.

Then get together as a team and appoint a new team leader. Spend thirty minutes identifying the top five strategies for your organization.

Worksheet 21

Empowerment Strategy

Strategy for Improving Empowerment	Support Structure for Assistance and Follow-Up

Taking the First Step Toward Empowerment

Due to the behavioral changes that are needed, it takes years to develop an empowered organization. Management must truly be willing to share meaningful power with the employee team, and the team must be responsible enough to effectively utilize this power. Both conditions must be present, and both management and the team must trust each other to function effectively.

Empowered Firms

- **Accomplish work through independent teams**
- **Foster an environment that develops, encourages, and rewards empowered people and teams**
- **Encourage people to build social and technical skills**
- **Align personal and organizational goals and see that people understand their roles**
- **Exhibit a high level of individual and team self-management**
- **Participate in work design, set direction, and resolve problems**
- **Provide people with the information they need—without asking**

An empowered organization accomplishes work through independent teams. Meaningful power is delegated to these teams to perform their work without the customary signature cycles, approval cycles, or waiting for other departments to perform their tasks.

Team empowerment often begins with small steps. Once an effective team is formed, with members who can work with one another, the team should agree that they will be responsible for certain tasks.

Team Empowerment

Team responsibilities:

69%	Safety and housekeeping
58	Assign task to members
53	Work with internal customers
46	Stop work for quality issues
45	Routine equipment maintenance
44	Vacation scheduling
42	Process improvements
38	Select work methods
34	External customers
33	Determine training needs
29	Set production goals

Monday Morning Mirror Issues

Teamwork --

Is a lot easier to talk about, than practice.

Some tasks should be shared with supervisors. That is, the team accepts supervisory input as guidance. Other tasks, such as compensation decisions, are often left for supervisors to perform.

Team Empowerment

Shared responsibilities:

54%	Select work methods
53	Determine training methods
51	Process improvements
49	Set production goals
44	Individual performance problems
44	Routine equipment maintenance
44	External customers

Supervisor responsibilities:

70%	Compensation decisions
55	Prepare and manage budgets
46	Performance appraisals
41	Individual performance problems

Monday Morning Mirror Issues

Who is the biggest enemy of teams?

Middle management. They have the most to lose.

However, it won't be easy. There are natural barriers to success. People who are used to working alone will now have to function together as a team. Supervisors who are used to controlling activities will have to change to more of a coaching style of leadership.

Barriers to Success

- **Personnel issues**
- **Supervisor resistance**
- **Transfer of power to teams**
- **Misalignment—compensation and team structure**
- **Difficulty with team members and supervisors in new roles**

See Kast and Laughlin, "Views on Self-Directed Work Teams." *Journal for Quality and Participation,* December 1990, pp. 48–51.

Empowerment teams have a process of "self-control" where the team assumes responsibility for its performance. A good way to visualize this is in terms of "results displayed," where the team reports (charts) a critical success factor.

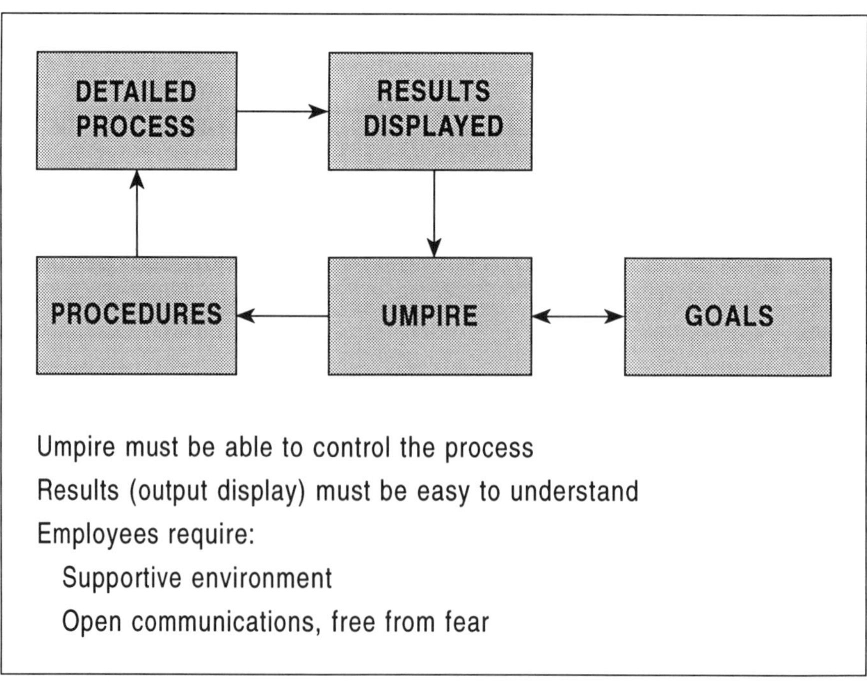

Self-Control: The Basis of Empowerment

Teams will accept and often welcome the opportunity to monitor critical quality factors because they recognize that high-quality goods and services are vital to their survival. Also, people have a natural inclination to try to achieve the highest possible quality in what they do.

Factors such as response time and number of units produced should not be reported in this self-control approach. People tend to view such reports as "work harder" programs. This viewpoint does not encourage teams to embrace the concept of quality improvement.

Management will have to assist the group in its step toward empowerment, which is to get control of its output. Without knowledge of its output quality levels, the group cannot correct its actions when necessary.

The following are examples of common output charts. The time period shown is a week, although daily or even hourly tracking might be required in some instances.

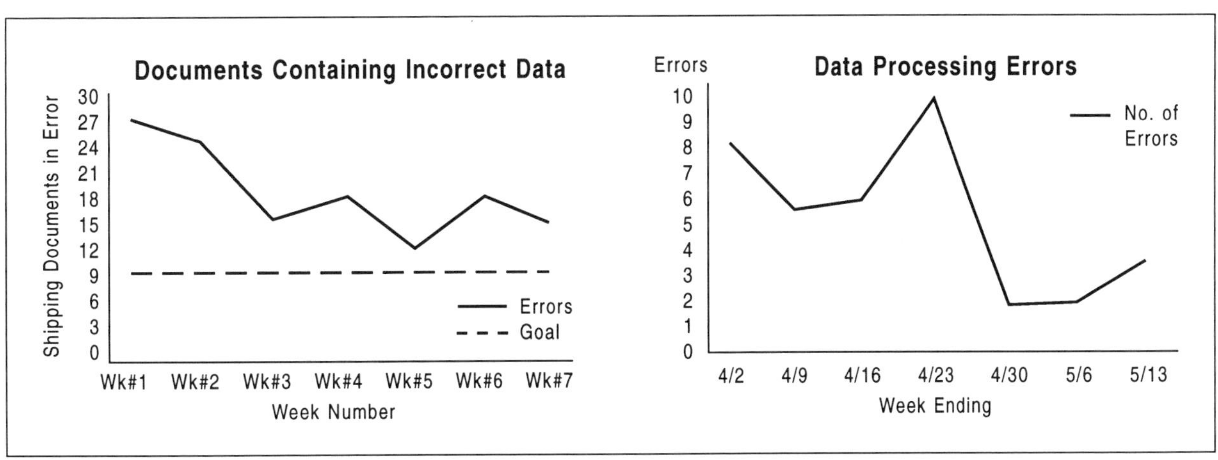

Also note that attention is centered on quality issues, such as the number of errors created. This technique cannot be used to encourage employees to work harder in terms of charting the number of units processed per time period. Nor is individual performance within the group being identified.

The objective of charting group output on a critical quality factor is to ensure that team members are aware of their quality levels.

When designing a developmental group empowerment system, concentrate on how the data will be captured (recorded). Inevitably, this will require a specialized form. This is typically the responsibility of an employee who is called the umpire. This function is rotated among all employees in the group, often on a monthly basis.

The empowerment comes about by asking the umpire to discuss what happened in a group meeting with the employees involved present. The point is not to highlight blame, but to openly discuss the process and what can be done to improve it.

The umpire observes the results displayed and makes adjustments to the process so that goals are met. Avoid the following common errors in your application:

- **An attempt to eliminate a problem**—Establish a continuous process whereby employees can see when an out-of-control condition occurs. Self-control is the key to continuous quality improvement.
- **A complex, broadly defined process**—The process must be a detailed subprocess that is well defined and fully understood.
- **Management involvement**—Should be none.
- **Complex goals**—If the goals are not simple and easy to understand, how can employees make corrections?
- **Broad phrases**—Be very specific.
- **Complex output display**—Display must be simple.

Monday Morning Mirror Issues

Being a useful team member
is not a job --

It is a commitment.

Exercise 22

Empowerment Application

Instructions:

Each participant is to spend ten minutes identifying a process and developing a sketch of the key quality factor (output) of the process. Using a real example, identify the time units on the X axis, and the output on the Y axis. That is, the team must be able to control the process by observing when a key quality factor does not conform to expectations.

Concentrate on developing a sketch of the results displayed (the output) by sketching your output on Worksheet 22.

After developing your graph, get back together in your assigned team. Be prepared to discuss how timely data are obtained for the key quality parameter being discussed.

Worksheet 22

Sketch and Graph of Output

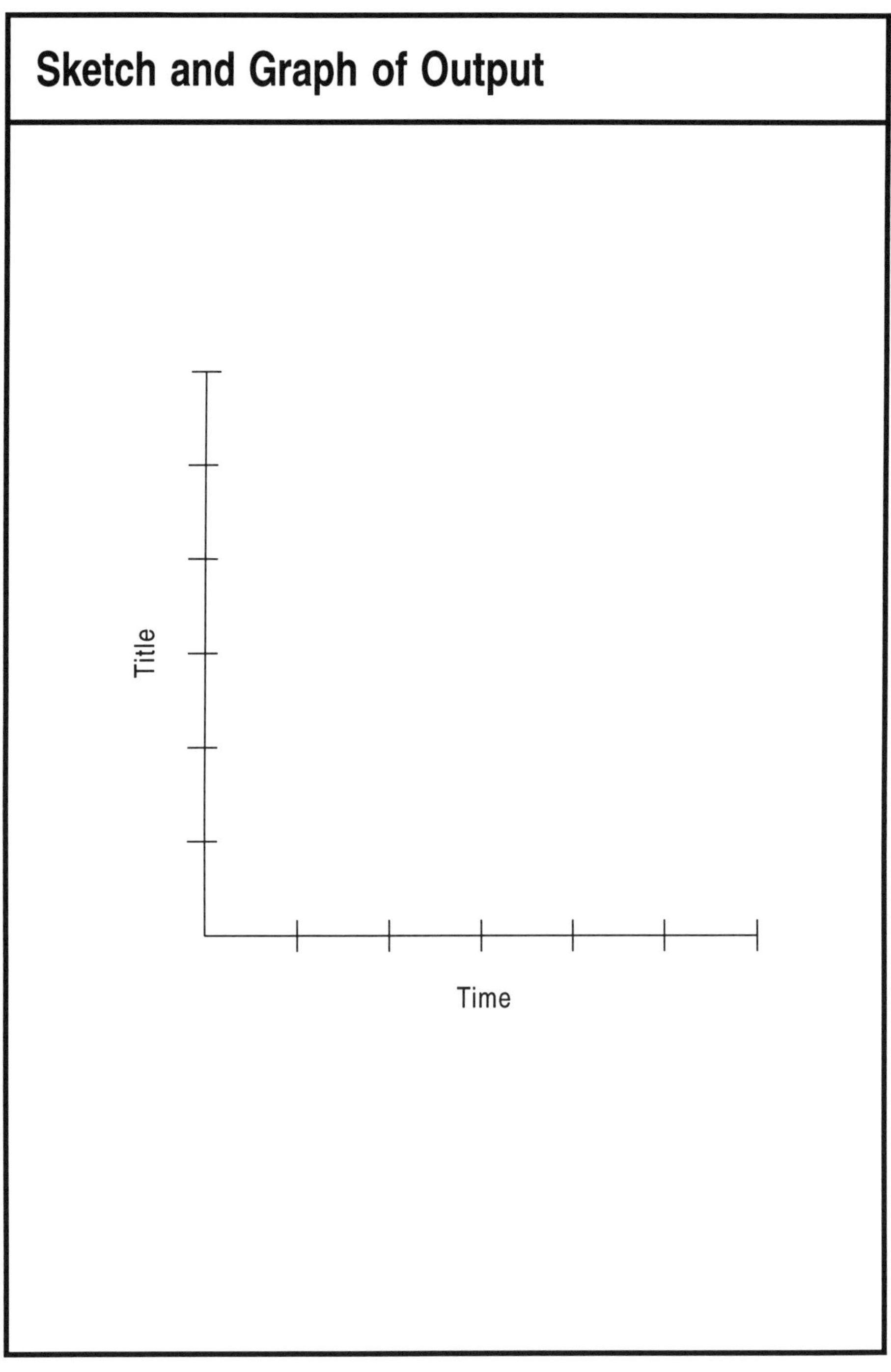

Empowerment Is Not Easy

Organizations frequently find empowerment to be a very difficult part of their quality initiative. This is due to several factors. First, management often has a "program-of-the-month" mentality, and what is "hot" this month, will not be the "in thing" next month and will have been forgotten by next year. Employees have learned to give "lip service" to new management initiatives, but continue to conduct business as usual.

The second problem with installing empowerment as an integral portion of the organizational culture is equally difficult to overcome. Many employees have previously tried creative initiatives on their own. They most likely failed, and a major reason why they failed was because they did not have an infrastructure (a quality council, if you will) to support them. They felt helpless in overcoming the organizational obstacles. The lesson gained from the experience might well be that they learned helplessness. That is, if they attempt something on their own, they will be helpless in overcoming obstacles.

The initial task undertaken by an empowered team should be one in which the team's success can be assured. There is a lot of negative learning to overcome, and this will take time and patience.

For additional information on problems with empowerment, read:

- G.M. Herrington, "The Catch-22 of Total Quality Management." *Across the Board,* September 1991, pp. 53–55.
- Roger McGrath, Jr. "Organizationally Induced Helplessness: The Antithesis of Empowerment." *Quality Progress,* April 1994, pp. 89–92.
- Lawrence Holpp, "Self-Directed Teams Are Great, But They're Not Easy." *Journal for Quality and Participation,* December 1993, p. 70.

Endnotes

1. For additional information, see "Leadership for Empowerment" by Spice and Alan Gilburg (*The Public Manager,* Fall 1992, pp. 27–31). The authors offer a collection of thoughts on this subject in an informative and thought-provoking article.
2. Source: "No Sense of Trespass: Empowerment through Informational and Interpersonal License" by Linda Martin and Judith Vogt (*Organization Development Journal*, Spring 1992, pp. 1–8).
3. The fourteen factors which Byham's study found to be common among empowered organizations were first reported in the April 1992 issue of *Quality Digest* (pp. 55–61) and have been updated periodically over the past two years. These factors have been used to demonstrate the notion that using management control to drive continuous improvement will fail in most cases.
4. It is not easy for employees to learn how to work together productively in empowered teams. A series of industry-specific team-building workbooks written by the authors are available from St. Lucie Press. Team-building skills are taught and reinforced by exercises which stress problems that will be encountered on the job. At the same time, teams practice a methodology by which they learn how to learn. The authors conduct quality improvement programs, including team-building programs, and can be reached through St. Lucie Press.

Exercise 23

It Wasn't My Fault, Officer

Instructions:

Suppose you had a car accident and the following groups had to perform their jobs correctly before you could drive your repaired car:

Police file accident report → Insurance agency paperwork → Adjuster reviews damages → Adjuster's office prices work → Body shop accepts estimate →

Repairs made to car → Adjuster verifies repairs → You accept car → You drive without problems

Consider the questions in Worksheet 23 in light of the above scenario.

Worksheet 23

Your Repaired Car

What is the probability of you driving your car, correctly repaired, without any problems if each group completes its part of the job correctly:

- 90% of the time?
- 95% of the time?
- 99% of the time?

What would be the effect on quality if the groups could be combined?

Chapter 9

Understanding the Consumer

An effective quality system must be focused on the consumer. The consumer includes both current customers and any potential customers. The consumer concept arose in marketing and is a market-driven concept that seeks out new opportunities.

The next three chapters deal with the consumer. First, we will review the concept of consumer orientation in terms of both external and internal consumers. Exercise 24 seeks ways to involve staff departments in the quality improvement system. Then, attention will be directed to measuring consumer satisfaction and attitudes. Exercise 25 consists of developing a brief questionnaire. Finally, when the attitudes have been identified, we will attempt to define consumer quality. Exercise 26 consists of identifying the quality of goods and services for a defined customer group.

The first step in a consumer orientation is for each group in the firm to define its customers in order to develop a personal involvement with the users or its services. Standard marketing demographics, such as age, sex, and income, tend to gloss over the in-depth understanding that is needed to understand customer needs.

Continuous quality improvement requires never-ending change and adaptation to meet the changing needs of the consumer. A consumer orientation is necessary to identify and monitor the perceptions that have an impact on the firm's success.

The problem with taking a consumer orientation is that the approach is complicated. Users of products and services (we will concentrate on the trickier aspect of service users) have both contractual and non-contractual expectations. Contractual expectations are those expectations which either are established in a contract or are so relatively tangible that consumers expect to receive them. Product quality is an example of a contractual expectation, as are reliability, dependability, and other product attributes. Also included in the contractual category of consumer service expectations are timely service and delivery of a certain category of items, among other factors.

Non-contractual expectations differ in that the consumer would receive something that surpasses expectations. Service delivered in a pleasant environment by a friendly, caring staff will go a long way toward surpassing consumer expectations.

Monday Morning Mirror Issues

How can I reduce department squabbles?

Elevate the importance of the customer.

Consumer Orientation

Match perceived expectations with perceived satisfaction

Contractual expectations:

- **Quality**
- **Service/product attributes**
- **Timeliness and delivery**
- **Physical location, etc.**

Non-contractual expectations:

- **Quality**
- **Expectation to satisfaction ratio**
- **Prestige, friendliness, environment**

Internal and External Customers

You have to identify and define your consumers before you can understand how they think. This is easier said than done in many firms because of the multitude of different consumers. An example of an external primary consumer is the buyer who actually uses your products and services. External secondary consumers (such as the family unit) may reinforce the buyer's satisfaction. Equally important, but often overlooked, are the internal consumers, or the users of the firm's support department services.

Consumer Orientation: Define Your Customers

External customer:

- **We identify with individuals**

Internal customers: Production

- **Regional sales manager**
- **User department**
- **User group**

Internal customers: Support departments

- **Accounting and Personnel have multiple customers**

Demographic segments of age, sex, and income are poor predictors of behavior

All departments must make a systematic effort to understand their consumers, and staff/support departments are no exception. When was the last time the accounting department asked you if its reports are readable? Many people do not use reports or budgets, despite the fact that such materials would enable them to do a better job, because the information was not prepared for their use.

When was the last time maintenance surveyed your employees to find out whether their services meet expectations. Undoubtedly, pure internal departments such as maintenance, human resources, and purchasing are often far removed from the external customer, but that is no reason for them not to make a systematic effort to identify the needs of users of their services. In a quality improvement system, every group must identify the needs of its consumers and work toward meeting those needs.

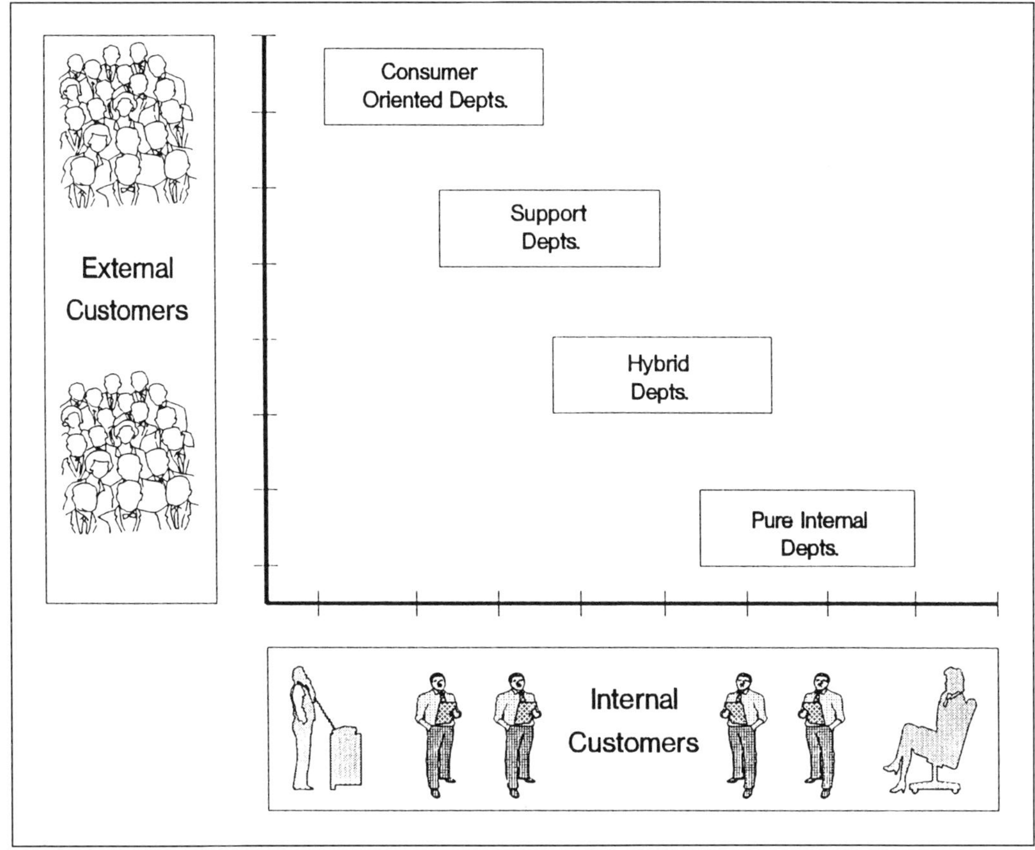

We must get close enough to our segment customer groups (i.e., treat each major customer group as a distinct entity) so that we can understand their expectations. Again, this can be very tricky. For example, a banking study conducted a few years ago revealed that consumers as a whole like to conduct their banking business in modern branch banks, with one major exception: parents with young children. These consumers did not like modern (defined as fancy) facilities because they felt ill at ease bringing their children, some of whom required constant attention, with them. Once this problem with a specific market segment was understood, bank personnel could brainstorm alternative ways to meet the banking needs of parents with young children (which in this case was to combine branch banks with supermarkets).

Consumer Orientation

- **Identify perceptions that have an impact on the firm's success**
- **Consumer/marketing linkages**—Before, during, and after service
- **Develop objectives for meeting consumer needs**
- **Assign responsibility for monitoring, reporting, and meeting objectives**
- **Group consumers based on similar perceptions**
- **Segments are not just economic**—Similar perceptual sets are better predictors of behavior

Monday Morning Mirror Issues

Sure, we must respond quickly to the needs of our market.

But what are our major market inhibitors?

Exercise 24

Involving Support Departments

Instructions:

Take ten minutes to identify two support departments and develop ongoing feedback systems they could install to improve the quality of their services. Using Worksheet 24, highlight the feedback system (such as surveys, interviews, brainstorming sessions, etc.) and how the system (feedback loops) could be used to demonstrate/improve customer satisfaction.

Note that attention is first directed toward identifying two support departments and their internal customers. What systems can the departments identified use to improve the quality of their service?

Attention is then directed toward identifying the two employee groups and the specific external customer groups they serve. What systems can these employee groups use to improve the quality of their services?

Then get together in your assigned team. Select two support departments for group discussion.

Worksheet 24

Internal Customers

Identify specific support departments and their internal customers. What systems can the departments install to improve the quality of their services?

External Customers

Identify two employee groups and the specific external customer groups they serve. What systems can be installed to improve service quality?

Chapter 10

Implementing a Consumer-Focused Measurement System

If you can't measure it, you can't manage it!

Peter Drucker

You have to identify who your consumer is before developing a system and associated surveys to measure and track consumer perceptions. Systems and surveys can only capture data on variables that you consider important. If you choose the wrong variables, the system and survey will give misleading results. For example, you could develop a survey to identify consumers' perceptions regarding their fingernails, but unless you are a beautician, the survey data will be of little use. Effective measurement systems are like tripwires, as the following story illustrates (adapted from a description of measures as tripwires in *Quality in Action* by Patrick Townsend and Joan Gebhard):

> From the first time that humans suspected that trouble might sneak up on them, tripwires have been used. They have a very specific, but limited, purpose. A tripwire tells you that there is trouble nearby and tells you approximately where to look. It doesn't tell you what to do, just where to look for the trouble that is on the way.
>
> If a troop of Scouts expect a raid by a neighboring group during a Jamboree, a literal tripwire may be strung across a likely path and attached either to a noisemaker or to someone's toe. In a coal mine, a canary is a tripwire measurement for poisonous gases. If the canary dies, miners

> know there is a problem. For most parents, a child's temperature serves as a tripwire measurement. If the child's temperature is normal, all is assumed to be well. If there is a fever, the alarm is sounded. Little specific information is gleaned, only that something needs attention.

A tripwire is a relatively low-cost diagnostic tool that signals an organization that a problem exists without immediately solving anything. Monthly statistics for on-time arrivals and baggage lost serve as tripwires for the airline industry. The fact that an airline's on-time rate dips from one month to the next doesn't really tell management anything about what solutions might be appropriate. It does, however, tell management that there is a problem and in which direction they should focus their efforts.

A well-designed set of tripwires makes it possible to apply constrained resources where needed most. No organization can monitor all contingencies all the time. The expenditure of resources would bring the company to its knees in short order. Thus, a corporate measurement system is quite simply a collection of tripwires designed to focus the organization on priority problem areas in need of attention.

Encamped armies often set tripwires at various distances from the heart of the camp. The devices don't stop the invaders, but they do give the defenders advance notice of an intruder's arrival. The earlier the impending trouble can be identified, the more time the leadership has to decide what to do about it and the better chance they have of committing exactly the right resources to solve the problem. Such an economical employment of people and material allows the leadership to have something left to face the next crisis.

Monday Morning Mirror Issues

Partial involvement in quality can only produce partial success --

Or total failure.

The same is true in business, where process measures often act as tripwires. The more sensitive the tripwires, the farther out they are, the more precise the company can be in deploying its resources to prevent severe problems, and the more capable it will be of handling more than one problem at a time. Rather than measuring every possible step of every possible process, a series of tripwires helps to define when more complicated statistical process control options need to be activated. You can't expect to achieve consistent results without precise measurements.

In a recent book by Aubrey Daniels entitled *Bringing Out the Best in People* (McGraw-Hill, 1994), the role of measures to reinforce and amplify positive and negative behavior is analyzed. Measurement tells us how much of the results and behaviors we are getting from the organization. The book also discusses the usefulness of graphic display for open communication and feedback, at least on the team level.

You need to know exactly what results you want and what acceptable behaviors will produce them. The measurement system helps to pinpoint both desired results and behaviors. Use it to define the precise results you want and the behaviors you require for achievement. Eight core elements are involved in the area of using a measurement system as a support structure for continuous quality improvement.

Map out functions and objectives/ products and services/customers and clients and their needs—This activity involves the interaction of the strategy and operations of the organizational unit for which the quality council has responsibility. The quality council is responsible for assuring that the functions of the operating area are in alignment with overall corporate strategy and direction. Teams are an ideal way to map out functions and processes to assure alignment and understanding. When assessing products and services, it is often helpful to think of each department as an independent (but interconnected) organization that is in business to provide products and services. By asking and answering the following questions, a clear starting point for creating indicators can be obtained:

- **Would I buy my services on the open market?**
- **How do I know?**
- **Can I compete as an entrepreneur?**
- **Am I running my department as a profitable and competitive enterprise?**
- **What are my key indicators of customer satisfaction and cost of providing services?**

Determine appropriate outcome and process indicators for each major function. There should be at least one outcome indicator for each major function. However, there can be many process indicators both within the function as well as cross functionally. Generally speaking, there are seven major categories around which outcome indicators can be built:

- **Customer/client satisfaction**
- **Accuracy of services**
- **Timeliness**
- **Responsiveness or speed**
- **Cost of services or products**
- **Safety of the environment**
- **Revenue or profitability**

Each major function should be analyzed to determine which outcome indices are appropriate. This will depend largely on the purpose or objectives of the function being performed. When identifying and building process indicators, it may be necessary to describe the process in terms of a flowchart, especially if one does not already exist. The goal is to develop a useful description of the process as it currently exists in order to identify key indicators and potential improvement areas. When building process indicators, it is important to look for interaction points among organizational units, as it is at these interaction points that problems frequently occur. It is usually best to start with current measures of the process, where available. By envisioning what a successful process looks like, missing indicators can be identified based upon the gaps and opportunities that exist. The key question to ask is, "How will the indicators help meet customer/client needs and improve operations?"

Link all indicators back to objectives—There are at least two ways to approach this activity: the short way and the linked way. The short way is to link all the indicators back to the corporate objectives. In many cases, this means forcing a fit or showing no fit because of the many gaps that exist. The linked way is to first develop department level/activity level objectives which are linked to corporate objectives. The department indicators are then linked to department objectives, thus creating a tight fit. The process of linking indicators to objectives helps assure that the right things are being measured and that they are being used to manage the operation.

Assign indicator owners—In most cases, the indicator owner should be the one person who either has the most ownership, has the most to lose, whose job accountabilities are most affected by good performance, or all of the above. The point here is that the indicator owner should have a major stake in the well-being of whatever the indicator measures.

Focus on areas of high priority and create targets and goals—When creating targets and goals in an objective manner, the following questions must be answered:

- **What are we facing? (situation analysis)**
- **What do we as a quality council want to happen? (objective setting)**
- **How are we going to get what we want? (alternative courses of action)**
- **What are the roadblocks and obstacles? (analysis of adverse consequences)**

The targets and their relationships to objectives (whether corporate or departmental) should be apparent. Operating plans that are developed should also link to the target/goal whenever possible.

Focus teams to eliminate obstacles and drive data gathering—The role of a measurement team can be very useful in breaking down the initial barriers and resistance. Team members should be representative of the areas being measured and should know where the data can be found. Getting reliable data to load into the department measurement system is often very time consuming and slow. Yet the task of collecting meaningful data is essential to good measurement. It is easy to combine data that should not be mixed, and the possibilities for error are endless.

Load data and assess specific areas of concern—A simple spreadsheet program can be used initially to load the historical data supporting the various measures being tracked. Data should be entered into the system on a weekly basis, or sooner if possible. A comparison to targets can be done monthly. Hopefully, targets can be expressed monthly as well to facilitate this comparison. Plans can then be developed to deal with longer term problems.

Provide corrective action—In an empowered organization, leadership involves group participation. Tight goals are sought by all levels and accepted both overtly and covertly. Strong pressure exists to get the facts and move swiftly toward corrective action, while keeping everyone who has a need to know informed.

Exercise 25

Creating Your Measurement System Strategy

Instructions:

Using Worksheet 25 as a springboard for ideas, develop the specific measurement system strategy that is best for your organization at this time. The measurement system should identify factors to track changes in consumer attitudes.

Take about ten minutes to record your ideas on Worksheet 25. Then spend about 20 minutes in a group discussion.

Worksheet 25

A Consumer-Focused Measuring System		
Key Factor to Be Measured	Frequency of Measurement	Support Structure

Evaluating Service/Staff Departments

> When you can measure what you are speaking about and express it in numbers, you know something about it, and when you cannot measure it, when you cannot express it in numbers, your knowledge is of a meager and unsatisfactory kind. It may be the beginning of knowledge but you have scarcely in your thoughts advanced to the stage of a science.
>
> *Lord Kelvin*

For years, the accounting and quality assurance functions have measured and tried to control the process that produces the products that will be delivered to your customers. As a result, great strides have been made in reducing direct product cost, while overhead costs have continued to increase at a rate that exceeds the reduction in direct costs. In most companies, the cost of poor quality in the service department runs 20 to 40% of the white-collar area's total budget. This means that you need to expand your continuous quality improvement activities from the manufacturing areas to service departments as well if your company is going to optimize its profits. To help put a stop to this runaway overhead cost, it is important that the quality system include white-collar service department measures of customer satisfaction.

In an effort to improve quality and reduce costs, some of the techniques that have proven effective in the manufacturing environment are now being applied to white-collar areas. In many companies, the business process is being viewed in much the same way as the product process. In most companies standard process control theory can be applied to more than 75% of the service business process. To accomplish this, the following steps should be taken:

1. **Define the critical service business processes.**
2. **Assign one person the responsibility for each critical service process.**
3. **Establish the beginning and end points for the service process.**
4. **Determine who the customers are and understand and document their expectations, needs, wants, and requirements.**
5. **Flow diagram the service process.**
6. **Define what inputs are required and develop specifications for each.**
7. **Establish appropriate measurements at process control points.**
8. **Develop feedback loops that provide individuals with feedback on their performance.**
9. **Implement an improvement process.**
10. **Document the lessons learned for other support departments.**

There are seven general or broad categories into which most types of service support department measures can be classified or rolled up: accuracy, responsiveness, timeliness, client satisfaction, cost, safety, and corporate responsibility. The first three—accuracy, responsiveness, and timeliness—refer to the manner and speed with which the support department conducts its business transactions.

The fourth category—client satisfaction—can also include employee satisfaction when employees are viewed as internal consumers. The fifth and sixth categories—cost and safety—can be broken down into a wide variety of subcategories. The final category—corporate responsibility—is often replaced in smaller departments with a more relevant category relating to the quality of work life. Point-of-service surveys can be used by support departments to create feedback on appropriate areas of measurement.

Survey Development

The most popular quantitative perceptual measuring instrument is called a Likert scale. This scale measures strength of agreement with a statement, ranging from 1 for strongly disagree to 7 for strongly agree.

Likert Scale

Simple instructions

Choose the number that best matches how you feel about each statement.

In my opinion:	**Strongly Disagree**			**Neutral**			**Strongly Agree**
Our town has nice weather most of the year	1	2	3	4	5	6	7

The scale measures strength of disagreement or agreement.

Survey objectives should be clearly specified before constructing statements for measurement. One-sentence objectives are best because they force a focus on exactly what you are trying to determine.

Survey Development

- **Clearly specify survey objectives**
- **Use one-sentence objectives such as:**

  Identify customer satisfaction with specific services
- **Brief, focused studies are best**
- **Identify major problem areas from the consumer's viewpoint (facilities, services received, etc.)**
- **Learn all you can about the subject**
- **Conduct extensive interviews**
- **Primary level: customers**
- **Support level: employees, mid/top management, receptionist, etc.**
- **Secondary level: accompanying friend, spouse**

After identification of the objective of the survey, statements designed to measure major aspects of the problem under study are generated.

Survey Development

- **Focus on one problem area at a time**
- **Generate statements covering the specific problem**
- **Think through how different groups might respond**
- **Cautions:**
  - Use simple wording
  - Eliminate compound stimuli
  - KISS (Keep It Simple, Stupid)
  - Be brief
  - Short, focused studies are best
- **Group statements into similar problem areas**
- **Identify key demographic questions**
  - Ask basic questions
  - Avoid personal questions

Avoid "creeping elegance" in surveys. A survey with a limited number of brief questions will receive more serious attention than a lengthy, multi-page questionnaire. All questions should be short and to the point. Compound phrases, such as "Our services are quick and easy to use," can confuse the respondent and should be avoided. Either break the phrase into two questions or, better yet, simply say: "Our services are easy to use."

Monday Morning Mirror Issues

Statistics never solve a problem.

They can only "point" people toward solutions.

Exercise 26

Your Perceptions of Quality

Instructions:

Spend a couple of minutes answering the questions on Worksheet 26 regarding your perceptions of quality. Then discuss your answers in the group. These are discussion questions, and as such there are no right or wrong answers.

Worksheet 26

Perceptions of Quality

Your Perceptions of Quality		
Quality Issues	**True**	**False**
Quality is an aspect of every job function.		
A manager's job is to solve problems.		
Employees do not have responsibility for decision making and problem solving.		
An inexpensive item is probably not a quality item.		
Quality is one aspect of the universal tradeoff between quality, schedule, and cost.		
If you pursue high quality, the product will cost as much as a Rolls-Royce.		
Our customers are not complaining; therefore our quality is high enough.		
I can prove levels of customer satisfaction.		
Employees should not take satisfaction surveys because the issues are too complex.		

Exercise 27

Measuring Perceptions

Instructions:

Get together in your assigned team and identify a specific internal support department. Then identify a key user of that support department's services. Finally, brainstorm information about the customer segment (users of the support department's services) that is need to make an informed decision about the quality of services delivered.

Brainstorm and complete the questionnaire in Worksheet 27 as a team project. Identify technical and "human" questions. Develop the specific demographic questions that should be asked. Your team leader will explain what you have developed to the larger group.

Worksheet 27

Measuring Perceptions

Definition of Consumer: ____________________________________

Objective of Study: ____________________________________

This questionnaire asks your opinion about issues regarding ________________ at our firm. Please choose the one number that best matches how you feel about the statement. The further away from the middle (4), the stronger your feeling about the statement.

For example, if you were asked about the quality of our food, and if you felt the quality was high but could be better, you might cross through the number "6" as shown:

	Strongly Disagree						**Strongly Agree**	**Unknown**
Our restaurant offers high-quality food.	1	2	3	4	5	~~6~~	7	0

IN MY OPINION:	**Strongly Disagree**						**Strongly Agree**	**Unknown**
1.	1	2	3	4	5	6	7	0
2.	1	2	3	4	5	6	7	0
3.	1	2	3	4	5	6	7	0
4.	1	2	3	4	5	6	7	0
5.	1	2	3	4	5	6	7	0
6.	1	2	3	4	5	6	7	0
7.	1	2	3	4	5	6	7	0
8.	1	2	3	4	5	6	7	0

Chapter 11

Defining Consumer Quality

The objective of this chapter is start thinking about quality from the consumer's viewpoint. Quality is a perceived attribute as determined by the consumer. It is the consumer's definition that counts; what we think is of secondary importance. If we are actually offering a high-quality service but the consumer doesn't like it, then by definition the quality is poor.

You can "toot your horn" and advertise that you have high quality, but be careful. If expectations are raised too high and consumers expect too much, they will be disappointed even if they are given a quality service. The trick is to position yourself so that you are perceived as a high-quality firm for a defined range of services. Thus, you avoid implying that you are "the best firm in the world."

Quality involves a perception (feeling) regarding a service (or a good) that is often held prior to use of the service. We mentally measure how well the service received stacks up against what we expected.

Defining Quality

- **Quality, like beauty, is in the eyes of the beholder.**
- **Service quality is a feeling that more was received than simply meeting specifications.**

- **Service quality is dependent upon the comparison of expected quality with the perception of what was actually received.**
- **High service quality occurs when the service received exceeds expectations.**

Thus, there are two major facets of consumer quality: the actual quality received and the quality level that is perceived. The actual quality is the objective quality measurement of the product (normally only products are measured in this depth). In measuring service quality, it is difficult to be more precise than a general agreement that the service is "reasonably good" or of "poor" quality. A common mistake that many firms make is to spend a huge amount of money on consumer research to find this "quality figure."

The expected quality is what the consumer expects to receive from use of the product or service. It is a purely subjective attribute and is heavily influenced by comments from friends and other users.

Defining Quality

Actual Quality:

- **The real level of quality provided**
- **Not the same as perceived quality**

Expected Quality:

- **What the customer expects upon arrival**
- **If expectations are too low, customers go elsewhere**
- **If expectations are too high, customers will not be satisfied—no matter how good the actual quality**

The perceived quality is what providers of goods and services must understand. Perceived quality is the customer's satisfaction. It is actual quality minus expected quality.

Defining Quality

Perceived Quality:

- **Actual quality – Expected quality = Customer's satisfaction**

Improving Perceived Customer Quality:

- **Employees become arrogant**
- **Must demonstrate care**
- **Use satisfaction surveys**
- **Customer is the star**
- **Invite customers to premises**
- **Train employees**
- **Respond to all complaints**

When was the last time you conducted a customer satisfaction survey?

Unfortunately, the argument does not end with measurement of perceived quality. The degree of customer contact comes into play. An example of a low-contact perception with a product or service would be tasting a product during a supermarket survey. You have an instant perception of the quality, but you do not weight your perception as heavily as you would with a high-contact use.

Dimensions of Quality Measurement of quality depends on degree of customer contact	
Customer Contact	**Attribute Measurement**
Low Contact	Supermarket survey: Taste this sausage. Does it taste good? Service department: Did we process you quickly?
Medium Contact	Customer satisfaction: Does your car run well days after repair? Are you satisfied? (questions are more personal)
High Contact	Quality of satisfaction: How well does the customer relate to the service? Define and test multiple points of interaction: service manager, mechanics, service facilities, etc.

Primary attention must be given to perceptions of perceived quality that are formed as a result of high contact with the service. However, such contact often occurs as the result of multiple points of service interaction. That is, perceived quality as the result of a perception derived from a single service point in the organization represents a meaningful measurement of quality.

Monday Morning Mirror Issues

Why is meeting customer expectations a losing strategy?

If the best you can do is meet expectations, then you have already lost the battle.

What if the perception of quality occurs as a user of hospital services (i.e., a patient) and is formed as a result of multiple points of interaction? The patient is serviced by the admissions department, orderlies, janitors, nurses, doctors, and, of course, food service. Each major point of interaction must be identified, and its impact on perceptions should be measured separately.

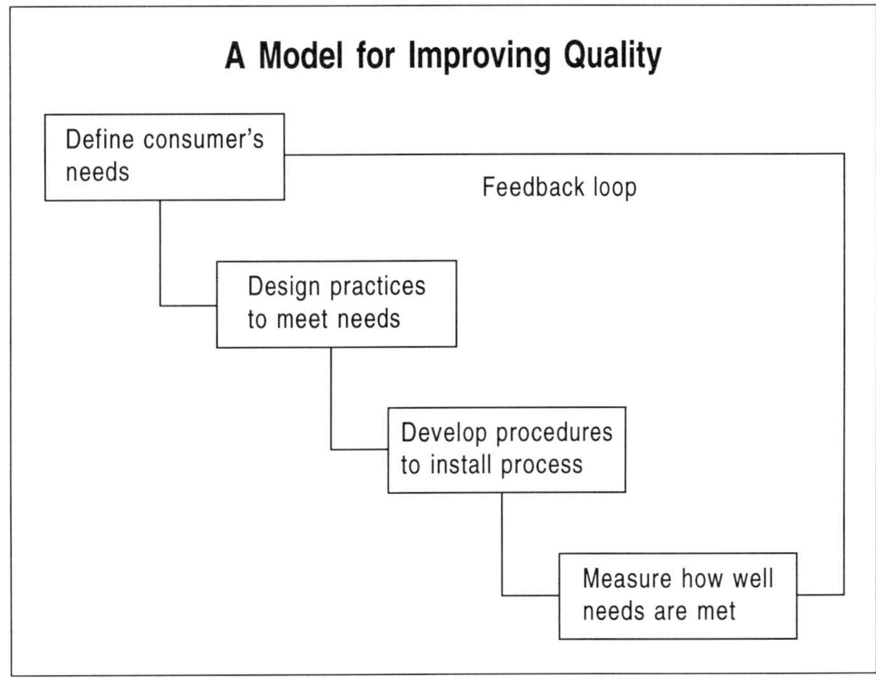

Perceived Quality = Actual quality – Expected quality

Perceived quality—Perceived quality is the customer's impression of what he or she has received. Consumers are satisfied if they feel that the actual quality received was more than they expected.

Actual quality—This is the real level of quality provided to the consumer as seen by the provider. Actual quality, particularly if product quality is being measured, is often expressed in hard numbers. A common mistake in measurement is to assume that actual quality is the same as perceived quality.

Expected quality—This is what the consumer expects. Advertising and word-of-mouth have a large influence on expected quality.

If expectations are too low, customers will go elsewhere. If expectations too high, customers will not be satisfied because no matter how good the actual quality is, they feel it should have been better (i.e., don't promise a "Garden of Eden").

Perceived quality (consumer satisfaction) and expected quality are soft numbers. They can be modified and/or changed.

Quality can be used as a competitive weapon, but it can backfire. If a firm promises more than it delivers, expected quality is raised. That is, since satisfaction is the perception of actual quality received above expected quality, satisfaction can actually decline if consumers expect too much.

- **Firms that forget their customers run the risk of failure**—Have you ever felt frustrated or insulted as a customer? Couldn't the problem have been solved?
- **When a firm ignores its customers, employees become arrogant, and sooner or later the customers leave.**
- **A firm must demonstrate concern for its customers.**
- **Get the consumer's point of view**—Use regular consumer surveys and distribute the findings.
- **Make the consumer the star of the show**—Escort key customers around the firm and introduce them to people.
- **Have an open house for employees and customers.**
- **Make sure each employee knows what his or her job means to the consumer.**
- **Respond to all complaints**—People who complain often want to continue dealing with the firm.
- **When did your firm last conduct a customer satisfaction survey or a survey of employee morale?**

What Is Quality?

A standard dictionary would define quality as follows: quality (kwal'ete) n., pl.-ties [<0Fr.<L.<qualis of what kind] 1. any of the features that make something what it is, characteristics, attribute; 2. basic nature, character, kind; 3. the degree of excellence which a thing possesses; 4. excellence, superiority; 5. [archaic] a) high social position; b) people of such position; 6. the property of a tone determined by its overtones, timbre.

Quality is more than meeting customer requirements—Sometimes it is a good idea to surprise your customer before your customer is surprised by one of your competitors. The following excerpt is from "Design for Total Quality":[1]

> A scientist who was in charge of a research lab asked sales representatives from three different companies to come and present their test equipment. The Hitachi salesman came and offered to run a test on some of the customer's actual materials on the very piece of equipment that would be delivered to him if he bought. He returned the test results the very next day. He made the sale and the equipment was delivered within the week. The other two salesmen were presented the challenge of matching the Hitachi service, but their system was not prepared to respond with this speed.

The customer did not have a requirement to see test results within 24 hours on the very piece of equipment he would purchase. This exceeded the customer's requirements and he was surprised by the quality of service. By establishing this new level of service, the Hitachi salesman created a new requirement in the management cycle for the other suppliers to match. He who establishes a new requirement is likely to leave his competitors behind.

Quality is anticipating, conforming to, and exceeding customer requirements—It is important that all employees understand that the world is in a state of dynamic change. Nothing stands still for long. Requirements are constantly shifting. Our expectations for computers, cars, homes, and personal services are dramatically different today than they were ten years ago, and the same will be true ten years from now. It is senior management's job to anticipate those requirements and design the quality system to respond to future requirements.

Quality as in *kaizen*-based total quality management—"...a process-oriented way of thinking (which) develops customer-focused strategies (to) assure continuous improvement involving people at all levels of the organizational hierarchy."[2]

Quality is continued improvement beyond the product and process and consists of total integrated continuous quality[3]—Every system of work has its outputs. Outputs are products or services. The goal of the management cycle is to go beyond optimizing the quality of products and services; focusing on the product or service itself is inadequate. Outputs are the result of a set of processes, and quality must be built into the process. The process of hiring and training employees may determine the quality of service in a restaurant. Concentrating on the service itself is too late in the flow of the process. Management quality must be built into the system, beginning with the creation of a vision and strategies and extended to the hiring process.[4]

Similarly, quality of a product is often determined during the design process for that product. Is it designed in a way that reduces the probability of variances in the manufacturing process? Do the materials specified reduce the variability in the manufacturing process? Has it been designed in a way that will meet the customer needs of tomorrow? Again, we can see that quality is largely a function of the process of work, as well as the management cycle, which consists of vision, strategies, planning, organizing, implementing, and controlling.

Job #1 is to continuously improve not only the product but the management cycle itself—Management-organized *kaizen* activities involve everyone in a company—managers and workers—in a totally integrated effort to improve performance at every level. This improved performance is directed toward satisfying such cross-functional goals as quality, cost, scheduling, manpower development, and new product development. It is assumed that these activities ultimately lead to increased customer satisfaction.[5]

There are many definitions of total quality control. One of the best was presented by Dr. Noriaki Kano in 1987: Total quality control is "a scientific, systematic and company-wide way of managing a business that emphasizes expansion of sales and growth of the company through achievement of customer satisfaction in its products and services." If we add the phrase "in the speediest possible manner," then the next definition is applicable.

Quality is related to speed—Every process can be measured in terms of both its output and the time required for the completion of the process, or its cycle time. Cycle time is a critical element in quality. Society has become conditioned to expect speed, whether in food service, car service, or telephone service.

Speed has another effect. The faster the cycle time, the higher the learning rate, and, therefore, the more continuous the improvement. It has long been understood by educators that the more frequent the quizzes and the more feedback to the student, the greater the learning. This is also true in business. The faster the service is provided to clients, the more opportunities to improve the process. The faster the process of product design, the more frequently that product can be redesigned to meet customer needs.

According to the Miller Consulting Group, there is one more critical aspect of speed. Speed and cost are directly related. The faster the cycle time, the lower the cost. Finally, they argue, the notion of cost and value must be considered if our understanding of quality is to be complete and forward thinking.

Quality leads to cost competitiveness—The Malcolm Baldrige National Quality Award and the European Quality Award have specifically recognized cost improvements as an element of quality. In the past, it was assumed that the production of a higher quality product or service required additional expense. While that was true when quality improvement was a result of increased cost being input into the system, we now know that true quality products cost less due to fewer rejects, rework, and other associated factors. The interesting paradox is that while quality products cost less, they can often be sold at a higher price. For example, a gold watch would necessarily cost more because of the high input cost. However, most customer requirements are met as a result of the process that transforms input to output. It is the system that produces quality.

When costs are driven out of the system, quality is improved. For example, Just-in-Time (JIT) inventory procedures and interruption-free manufacturing processes reduce the costs of goods in process. However, they also tend to improve quality. They improve quality when the entire system is designed to eliminate interruptions by placing responsibility at the first level, where employees take responsibility for quality by doing their jobs right the first time. JIT cannot succeed if an employee must check out the decision to reject a bad part with his or her manager, who in turn must check with quality control, etc.

The more checks, the less individual responsibility, the slower the system, and the lower the quality. Thus, going beyond product and into the integrated continuous quality improvement areas is where the breakthroughs of the future will be found.

A quality organization is wealth creating—Business fulfills many noble purposes in society. The social purpose is the creation of real wealth, for real wealth is created when a new product or new service is created. This creates new jobs and adds wealth to the aggregate of society.

Wealth building is a creative act. It is the result of human initiative and risk taking. Dr. Deming's Fourteen Points include "drive out fear." Why is it important to drive out fear? Fear is the nemesis of both quality and creativity. A person who lives in an environment of control through fear does not experiment, initiate, or create and avoids risk.

The revolution in the bureaucratic communist states of Eastern Europe and the Soviet Union is a revolution against fear. These societies have not been wealth creating because their citizens have been controlled through fear and, therefore, have avoided the risks of creativity. They have developed the habits of avoiding the very risks that are required to create wealth.[6]

Similarly, bureaucratic companies drive out quality and creativity, destroying the wealth-creating mechanism of human initiative and risk taking. A quality management organization builds wealth through the integration of human initiative within the management cycle.

Exercise 28

Defining Consumer Quality

Instructions:

Get together in your assigned team. Using Worksheet 28, identify a customer segment and a service your organization delivers to that segment. Technically, we are trying to understand this segment's perception of the quality received, but it is unlikely that we have the data to do so.

Brainstorm the factors and data needed to identify the actual quality and the expected quality of this customer segment. Your team leader will explain the team's ideas to the larger group.

Worksheet 28

Defining Consumer Quality

Quality Worksheet

Customer Segment:

Service Delivered:

Actual quality factors and data needed:

Expected quality factors and data needed:

Endnotes

1. Lawrence M. Miller, "Design For Total Quality," The Miller Consulting Group, 1991, p. 14.
2. Masaaki Imai, *Kaizen: The Key to Japan's Competitive Success,* The Kaizen Institute, Ltd., 1986, p. 5.
3. "After Product Quality in Japan: Management Quality, by Seiichiro Yahagi (*National Productivity Review,* Autumn 1992, pp. 501–515), was rated one of the most important new articles to come out of Japan in 1992. The author proposes the use of expert systems featuring a 12-factor model. The system is organized into 41 "elements" of measurement subfactors. Japanese management has moved beyond product quality, the author states, to an emphasis on total integrated management (TIM)—management concerned about each facet of the company and interrelating all the facts into a concerted, comprehensive corporate management policy of innovation. The author has developed an expert system which measures the 12 factors that determine management quality, divided into 41 subfactors, of which he sees 6 factors as critical to the success of a company. The foremost of these 6 is the management cycle, with vision being the driver.
4. Miller and his associates advocate that the "whole systems" process of planning the total quality organization is a breakthrough because it is a different way of thinking about change. See "Design For Total Quality," pp. 15–16.
5. Masaaki Imai, *Kaizen: The Key to Japan's Competitive Success,* The Kaizen Institute, Ltd., 1986, p . XXV.
6. For further discussion of this topic, see Peter Drucker, "The New Society of Organizations," *Harvard Business Review,* September/October 1992, pp. 95–104.

Chapter 12

Improving Services

Ten years ago, Michael P. Quinn, assistant vice-president at Manufacturers Hanover Trust Company, reported, "Continuous Quality Improvement is a methodology which can be applied by banks and other financial institutions to reduce their total costs while at the same time increasing the productivity of the operation."

Quinn's presentation at that time showed that opportunity costs associated with quality in banks can range from 15 to 40% of a department's total operating expenses. These numbers have since been verified by studies conducted on the cost of quality over the past ten years.

A 1987 accounting study of the Federal Reserve Bank of Philadelphia as presented by Morse and associates is an indicator that quality systems usually are not as well developed for service organizations as they are for manufacturing organizations. Morse does state, "Continuous Quality and quality cost concepts are just as applicable to services as they are to physical products."

John F. Akers, former president of IBM, stated on March 13, 1984, "Our studies show that more than 50 percent of the total cost of billing relates to preventing, catching or fixing errors."[1] Yet ten years later, many of these problems are still unresolved, and IBM stock hovers near a ten-year low.

For years, the accounting and quality assurance functions have measured and tried to control the process that produces the products that will be delivered to customers. As a result, great strides have been made in reducing direct product cost while overhead costs have continued to increase at a rate that exceeds the reduction in direct costs. In most companies, white-collar poor-quality cost runs 20 to 40% of the white-collar area's total budget. This means that you need to expand your continuous quality improvement activities from the manufacturing areas if your company is going to optimize its profits. To help put a stop to this runaway overhead cost, it is important that the quality system include white-collar quality costs.

Service Improvement Ideas

In an effort to reduce quality costs, some of the techniques that have proven effective in the manufacturing environment are now being applied to white-collar areas. In many companies, the business process is being viewed in much the same way as the production process. In most companies, standard quality process control theory can be applied to more than 75% of the business process. To accomplish this, the following steps should be taken:

1. **Define the critical business processes.**
2. **Assign one person the responsibility for each critical business process.**
3. **Establish the beginning and end points for the process.**
4. **Determine who the customers are and understand and document their expectations.**
5. **Flow diagram the process.**

6. **Define what inputs are required and develop specifications for each.**
7. **Establish appropriate measurements at process control points.**
8. **Develop feedback loops that provide individuals with feedback on their performance.**
9. **Implement an improvement process.**
10. **Standardize and seek opportunities for replication.**

A quality system is an important part of such service industry areas as banking, health care, personnel training, public utilities, and government. In his book *Applications of Quality Control in the Service Industries,* A. C. Rosander reports that 25% of a bank's total operating costs are devoted to poor quality costs. He estimates that the opportunity is broken down in the banking industry as follows:

Prevention savings	2%
Appraisal savings	28%
Internal error savings	41%
External error savings	29%

Monday Morning Mirror Issues

The only person in the world who wants to be changed --

Is a baby.

John Heldt, a consultant who has assisted many companies in implementing their continuous quality systems, states, "Reducing the cost of poor quality will increase your overall profit more than doubling sales." He adds, "Most companies are spending more than three times as much for poor quality as they are making in profit. Cut your poor-quality cost in half and you will at least double your profit."[2] Doubling production requires a major financial investment—more people, more equipment, more materials, more floor space, more support personnel, more sales personnel, more managers—more of just about everything. For every dollar that poor-quality cost is reduced, a dollar is directly added to the profit margin.

Continuous quality improvement should be used as a tool to help management direct today's activities and plan for the future. It provides a measurement tool that helps quantify how effective past activities were. It provides data that can be analyzed to pinpoint major problem areas. It provides the information needed to budget realistically. It also helps management prepare meaningful cost estimates for new products, services, or businesses.

Monday Morning Mirror Issues

The only time I bring people into my office is when there is a problem. Am I building confidence?

No. You are building terror.

Exercise 29

Developing a CQI Strategy for Service Departments

Instructions:

The following is a synopsis of the various reasons for and benefits of using a continuous quality improvement system in service operations. Use Worksheet 29 to develop your own CQI strategy for your service departments.

1. CQI provides a manageable entity.
2. CQI provides a single overview of quality. It allows the total company quality situation to be summarized and viewed in one common concept.
3. CQI provides a means of measuring change. It provides a way of finding the best interim operating point for the quality system.
4. CQI provides a problem-prioritization system. Frequently, the most visible problem or even the one that occurs most frequently is not the one whose solution has the biggest payback.
5. CQI aligns quality and company goals. It assures that the quality goals are aligned with company goals and objectives.
6. CQI provides a way to correctly distribute controllable poor quality cost for maximum profits.
7. CQI brings quality into the boardroom. It makes for effective communication between the quality staff and upper management.
8. CQI provides for effective use of resources.
9. CQI provides new emphasis on doing the job right every time.
10. CQI helps to establish new management leadership processes.
11. CQI provides a measure of improvement. It provides the best measure of the effectiveness of a company's continuous improvement process.
12. CQI is one of the best ways to increase a company's profits.

Every poor-quality cost dollar that is spent takes away directly from the bottom line. Eliminating this waste is an objective of CQI.

Worksheet 29

Service Department Rationale	
Benefit/Reason for Doing	Action Items of Importance

Get the Right People to Deliver Service

Job descriptions for customer contact employees are usually not written in terms of quality services.

In a firm with superior services, all jobs are tied to the delivery of quality services, either directly or indirectly, to support the staff responsible for quality services. The reason this is not done more often is because it is easier to evaluate typing skill (60 words per minutes) than it is to determine that phone calls are answered so that the caller feels satisfied that his or her call has been handled professionally, pleasantly, and efficiently.

Training provides some skills, but some qualities must exist within the individual. Courteous, pleasant, outgoing personalities are needed. Consider the recruitment approach taken at Disney World, where an applicant auditions for a role rather than applies for a job. This sends a message to the job applicant as to what the job is about and the skills and attitudes needed.

Create an Organization that Fosters Service

- **Management by walking around—visit service delivery locations**
- **Consider service quality in promotions and job enrichment**
- **Front-line service personnel need to ask themselves:**
  - **Do I know my firm's quality policy?**
  - **How often do I contribute improvement/quality ideas?**
  - **Do I volunteer for assignments that will allow me to improve the quality of our goals and services?**

Firms cannot leave customer satisfaction to chance. Suppose you were a customer. What services most offend you?

Examples of Confused Priorities

- **Marketing develops and advertises a new product and service, but customer contact personnel are not informed.**
- **A service person finishes his conversation with a friend while you wait to be served.**
- **Service personnel do not recognize or acknowledge a steady customer.**

See Linda Lash's book, *The Complete Guide to Customer Service* Wiley, New York, 1989), for a complete discussion of this topic.

Gap Analysis

Gap analysis[3] is a method used to identify perceptions held by various groups regarding your services, so that you can determine the distance (gap) between the groups. That is, customer expectations seldom match management perceptions. However, if you can develop an understanding of in which specific subfactors (issues) gaps exist, then you can work to close those gaps.

Gaps can exist in traditional aspects of quality such as time, quality, schedule, flexibility (ability to adapt to requests), courteousness, attitudes, or a host of other factors.

Types of Service Gaps

Gap 1: Customers' expectations–management's perceptions

Customer Expectations
Gap 1
Management Perceptions

Gap 2: Management's perceptions of customers' expectations of service quality

Service Quality Specifications
Gap 2
Management Perception of Service Delivery

Gap 3: Service quality specs and service delivery

Service Delivery
Gap 3
Service Quality Specifications

Gap 4: Service delivery and external communications (i.e., promises)

Service Delivery
Gap 4
External Communications

Gap 5: Customer expectations of service offered and service received

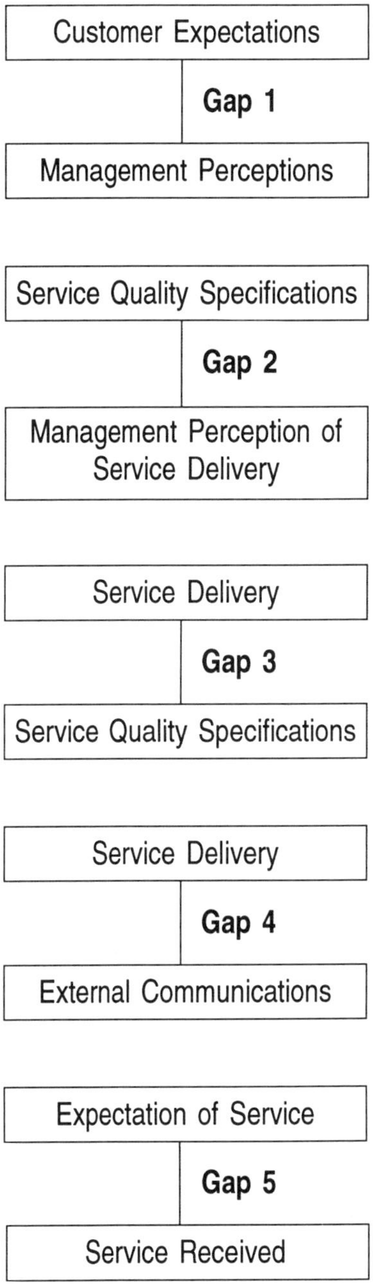

Expectation of Service
Gap 5
Service Received

Endnotes

1. John F. Akers, remarks at American Electronics Association Seminar on Quality, Boston, March 13, 1984.
2. John J. Heldl, personal communication, October 14, 1986.
3. For a complete discussion of gap analysis, see Valarie A. Zeithamal, A. Parasuraman, and Leonard L. Berry, *Delivering Quality Services,* The Free Press, New York, 1990.

Monday Morning Mirror Issues

Why is it that some people learn from their experience, and --

Others never recover.

Exercise 30

Closing Service Gaps

Instructions:

A small firm has just completed a CQI development program and has decided to apply the concept of gap analysis to the three areas shown below. Break into teams and take fifteen minutes to identify what can be done to close the gaps. Use Worksheet 30 to record your ideas. Your team leader will explain your findings to the group.

Accounting Department

Accounting management: We provide all departments with accurate and timely reports.

Internal departments: We don't see reports. But, we don't have much use for accounting reports.

Facilities Management

Facilities manager: We keep the firm as clean as possible considering the low budget we receive.

Employees: Our offices are rather dirty and somewhat dingy. But that's okay; it's a nice place to work.

Customer Service Department

Management: We provide high-quality services at a low cost that customers cannot get locally.

Customer: I have to wait weeks for repairs, and they charge a fortune.

Worksheet 30

Closing the Gaps

Closing the Gaps in:

Accounting Department:

Facilities Management:

Customer Service Department:

Exercise 31

No, That's Not True

Instructions:

In order to understand the potential of gap analysis, everyone's cooperation will be needed in role playing. First, the group as a whole is to identify two customer segments serviced by your organization which will be examined using gap analysis. These two customer segments should be written on a board (or flip chart).

If there are enough participants, divide the group into four teams (A/B and C/D). If there are not enough participants, divide the group into two teams (A and B). Go to teams A and B and flip a coin. If it's heads, assign team A to customer segment #1 and team B to customer segment #2. If it's tails, assign team A to customer segment #2 and team B to customer segment #1. Do with same with teams C and D.

Record the team assignments and the factors (gaps) developed on Worksheet 31. Ask each team to go to a separate area to perform a gap analysis. Each team has twenty minutes to apply gap analysis to identify customer expectations and management perceptions for their assigned customer segment.

In defining customer expectations, each team is to take the position of a consumer's union that is openly "anti-business" They are "out for "blood" and hold an extreme view on each of the factors. They are to take minor points and blow them out of proportion in their attempt to win their argument. Each team's position will be determined by the flip of a coin. That is, when the teams return, if the flip of a coin is heads for team A, then team A will be assigned the position of presenting gap analysis from the strong viewpoint expressed by the consumer's union. Team B has the dual responsibility of first answering team A's viewpoint and presenting their own managerial viewpoint. After teams A and B present their views, ask teams C and D to suggest what can be done to close the gaps identified.

After a discussion on closing the gaps, teams C and D take their turn. If the flip of a coin is heads for team C, then team C will be assigned the position of presenting the gap analysis from the strong viewpoint expressed by the consumer's union. Team D has the dual responsibility of answering team C's viewpoint and presenting their own managerial viewpoint. After teams C and D present their views, ask teams A and B to suggest what can be done to close the gaps identified.

Worksheet 31

Gap Analysis

Gap Analysis:
Customer Expectations versus Management Perceptions

Customer Segment #:

Customer expectations:

Management perceptions:

Exercise 32

The Dreamer

Instructions:

Mr. Tom Swartz, president of a small local firm, has just completed a management development program to identify systems that will be needed to install and support continuous quality improvement. It was an exhausting program during which several new ideas were presented. After dinner, he tries to recall some of the more important points, but becomes sleepy.

Tom sits down in his easy chair and begins thinking that he needs an "ideal firm" which offers idealistically perfect service, regardless of the cost. If he could identify such a firm and its host of services, he would have an image of what to work toward.

If only he could envision such an idealistically perfect firm, with fully satisfied customers. If only he could identify the procedures that would be needed. If only he could envision what the customer would experience in dealing with such a firm. If only...and he falls asleep.

Get together in your assigned team. Using Worksheet 32, you have twenty minutes to select a service offered by your firm and complete Tom's dream. That is, for a specific customer segment, identify the idealistically perfect service the firm or department could offer, regardless of the cost of the service. Your team leader will explain your findings to the larger group.

Worksheet 32

The Dreamer

Customer Segment:

Service Offered:

Service Factors:

Chapter 13

Quality Systems: ISO and Baldrige

Developing quality systems, particularly systems designed to improve service quality, is difficult. Service quality is inherently variable, and conformance to standards may not be enough (i.e., see measuring perceptions).

Service Quality

- Dependent upon human factors
- Behavior
- Personality
- Perception
    - Inherently variable
    - Cannot be inventoried
    - "Moment of truth" complexities
    - Environment
    - Competence
- Production/consumption may be combined
- Conformance often is not enough

Furthermore, service tends to operate in a relatively non-competitive environment. For example, if you want to buy a consumer product, whether a toaster or a car, you can do so in an objective manner. Look up the product in *Consumer Reports,* identify which two brands have the best quality, go to a store or dealer, price the brands, and buy the cheapest.

It is extremely difficult to be precise with service quality. Definitions of service quality are unclear, and development of measurements for service quality has been slow. The Baldrige criteria offer guidance with issues that involve consumer satisfaction and how these measurements should be deployed throughout the organization. ISO quality standards (more on this in a moment) devote minimal attention to satisfaction measures and concentrate on one aspect of quality: the management of process quality. Documentation in the form of a quality manual and procedures are stressed as a means of controlling process quality.

Monday Morning Mirror Issues

The Baldrige system is too complex for our organization.

So, pick and choose a couple of ideas to work on.

Service Quality Weaknesses and Problems

- Unclear definitions: quality, system
- Delivery processes not well defined, contribute to variability
- Lack of quantitative foundation, internal measures
- Lack of benchmarking
- Lack of strategy, design, and infrastructure (reaction instead of prevention)
- Difficulty in:
  - Control
  - Assurance
  - Assessment
  - Comparison
  - Prediction
- Not adequately reflective of operating in a competitive environment

Using the Baldrige Criteria

The Baldrige Award identifies quality in terms of manageable subportions. The real value of the award is in the criteria, which assist managers in identifying quality factors and in deploying those factors throughout the organization. Frankly, reporting on all the award criteria would "swamp" most managers. So much time would be spent developing quality reports that there would be little time left for management to do its basic job unless staff assistance was provided.

Employees will most likely point out this reporting problem, often in less than polite terms. However, unless some positive action is taken to identify specific factors that influence quality and progress on the factors identified is recorded, quality has not been brought under control.

The Malcolm Baldrige National Quality Award criteria are explained in a fifty-page document. At first glance, this document is often intimidating. Therefore, a simplified quality needs assessment questionnaire has been developed using the Baldrige Award criteria. This questionnaire, shown on the following pages, can be used as a guide in evaluating your organization for strengths and areas for improvement.[1]

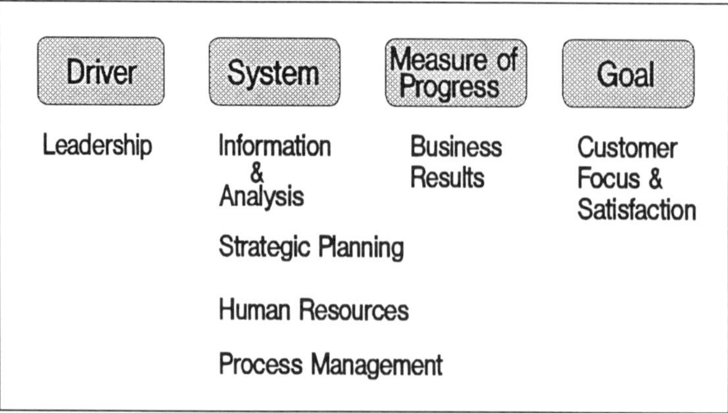

The Baldrige Award Structure Provides a System for CQI

Quality Needs Assessment

This questionnaire asks your opinion about issues regarding quality. Please choose the one number that best matches how you feel about the statement.

LEADERSHIP **In my opinion:**	**Strongly Disagree**						**Strongly Agree**
1. Our firm has a known quality policy.	1	2	3	4	5	6	7
2. Employees know our quality goals.	1	2	3	4	5	6	7
3. Management is visibly involved in developing a quality culture.	1	2	3	4	5	6	7
4. Management is trained in quality concepts.	1	2	3	4	5	6	7
5. Management practices quality concepts.	1	2	3	4	5	6	7
6. Quality responsibilities have been clearly communicated to all employees.	1	2	3	4	5	6	7
7. Quality committees coordinate between departments.	1	2	3	4	5	6	7
8. The community knows our quality goals.	1	2	3	4	5	6	7
9. Adequate resources are provided for quality improvement.	1	2	3	4	5	6	7
INFORMATION AND ANALYSIS **In my opinion:**							
10. Our firm reports data on all important dimensions of customer quality.	1	2	3	4	5	6	7
11. Our firm reports data on all important service dimensions.	1	2	3	4	5	6	7
12. We know what our competitors are doing.	1	2	3	4	5	6	7
13. We analyze data on our suppliers' view of our quality.	1	2	3	4	5	6	7
14. Data are used to analyze our performance.	1	2	3	4	5	6	7
15. We identify the causes of poor quality.	1	2	3	4	5	6	7

STRATEGIC PLANNING **In my opinion:**	**Strongly Disagree**						**Strongly Agree**
16. We use competitive data from other firms when developing quality goals.	1	2	3	4	5	6	7
17. We have an operational plan (1–2 year) that describes our quality goals.	1	2	3	4	5	6	7
18. Our employees are involved in quality planning.	1	2	3	4	5	6	7
19. We have specific methods for monitoring progress toward improving quality.	1	2	3	4	5	6	7
20. There are quality plans in effect for all departments.	1	2	3	4	5	6	7
21. We have quality plans for our suppliers.	1	2	3	4	5	6	7

HUMAN RESOURCE DEVELOPMENT AND MANAGEMENT
In my opinion:

22. We have a known plan to involve employees in quality improvement.	1	2	3	4	5	6	7
23. Quality criteria are used in employee performance evaluations.	1	2	3	4	5	6	7
24. Quality goals are communicated to all employees.	1	2	3	4	5	6	7
25. Our employees believe in the seriousness of providing top-quality services.	1	2	3	4	5	6	7
26. All employees are trained in quality improvement concepts.	1	2	3	4	5	6	7
27. We reward employees for their quality improvement efforts.	1	2	3	4	5	6	7
28. Our firm collects data on employee morale.	1	2	3	4	5	6	7
29. Training effectiveness is evaluated.	1	2	3	4	5	6	7

PROCESS MANAGEMENT **In my opinion:**	**Strongly Disagree**						**Strongly Agree**
30. Customer quality expectations are defined.	1	2	3	4	5	6	7
31. Customer requirements are transferred into the planning process for improvements.	1	2	3	4	5	6	7
32. We evaluate our processes for improvement.	1	2	3	4	5	6	7
33. Cycle times have been reduced for key processes.	1	2	3	4	5	6	7
34. Support departments have defined quality goals.	1	2	3	4	5	6	7
35. Documents showing our quality are kept up to date.	1	2	3	4	5	6	7
36. Competitive data are used in making process improvements.	1	2	3	4	5	6	7
37. We work with suppliers to improve quality.	1	2	3	4	5	6	7

BUSINESS RESULTS* **In my opinion:**							
38. Our customer response time has improved.	1	2	3	4	5	6	7
39. We can demonstrate that we have improved our quality in the last three years.	1	2	3	4	5	6	7
40. We can demonstrate improvements in quality by our support departments.	1	2	3	4	5	6	7
41. We can demonstrate improvements in quality by our suppliers.	1	2	3	4	5	6	7
42. There has been a decrease in customer complaints in the last three years.	1	2	3	4	5	6	7

* Financial results are also reported in this category, including the effective use of capital and assets. Organizations are encouraged to benchmark themselves on key performance measures such as labor turnover, safety, and environmental improvements.

	Strongly Disagree						Strongly Agree
43. We have developed several new products and services in the last three years.	1	2	3	4	5	6	7
44. We use independent firms to compare our products and services with key competitors.	1	2	3	4	5	6	7

CUSTOMER FOCUS AND SATISFACTION
In my opinion:

45. Our customers like the quality of our services.	1	2	3	4	5	6	7
46. Customer satisfaction data are reported by customer groups.	1	2	3	4	5	6	7
47. We can prove we have higher levels of customer satisfaction than our competitors.	1	2	3	4	5	6	7
48. Customer complaints have decreased.	1	2	3	4	5	6	7
49. Our job definitions encourage our employees to quickly resolve customer complaints.	1	2	3	4	5	6	7
50. We use innovative approaches in assessing customer satisfaction.	1	2	3	4	5	6	7

Exercise 33

Baldrige Consultant

Instructions:

Get together in your assigned team and appoint a new team leader. Take ten minutes to individually read over the following mini-case. Identify what you feel are the two areas of greatest strength, the two areas in need of improvement, and what could be done to improve the firm's quality processes. Record your findings on Worksheet 33.

After completing your analysis of Ajax Industries using the Baldrige criteria, get together in your assigned team. Try to reach general agreement on the strengths and areas for improvement. Brainstorm what could be done to improve the process. Where should Ajax begin the improvement process? Why?

Baldrige Mini-Case:

A consultant is hired to audit the quality control processes at Ajax Industries, a medium-sized service firm. The consultant uses selected questions from the Baldrige Award to privately survey 300 employees.

Answers (response means) to selected questions are shown. Analyze the responses, and highlight the firm's strengths and weaknesses.

	Strongly Disagree ... Strongly Agree 1 2 3 4 5 6 7
Our firm has a known quality policy statement.	2.8
The community knows of our quality goals.	1.7
Our firm reports data on all important service dimensions.	3.2
We identify the cause of poor quality.	5.9
Competitive data from other firms are used when developing quality goals.	1.9
Our employees are involved in the quality planning process.	3.0
Our employees believe in the seriousness of providing top-quality services.	6.1

Worksheet 33

Baldrige Consultant's Analysis

Two greatest strengths:

Two areas for improvement:

How would you improve the areas identified?

Exercise 34

Can We Use Any of the Baldrige Criteria?

Instructions:

Reread the section on the Baldrige Award. Take particular note of the questions shown in the quality needs assessment questionnaire.

Get together in your team. Select one of the seven major award categories that you feel merits consideration by your firm. Then, choose or modify any of the questions within the award category selected.

When selecting questions within an award category, ask yourself how reporting against the questions would enhance quality improvement. Spend twenty minutes reaching consensus on the questions to be asked. Remember, keep it simple, and avoid "creeping elegance" when selecting your questions.

Worksheet 34

Baldrige Award Factors

Major category selected:

Specific reporting factors within the category:

What Are the ISO Standards?

The Geneva-based International Organization for Standardization (IOS) first published a series of standards in 1987. These standards became known as the ISO (meaning equal) standards. They provide a basis on which a registered company could assure buyers of its capability of producing quality goods.

The term "ISO" describes the series of international standards that deal with product design, production, delivery, service, and testing. A series of five ISO standards (ISO 9000, 9001, 9002, 9003, and 9004) describe the elements for establishing and maintaining a quality management system. A company registered as complying with ISO standards has demonstrated to an accredited registrar that its processes have met the standards expressed in ISO 9001, 9002, or 9003.

Overview of ISO Standards

Std #	Title	Function
9000	**Quality management and quality assurance standards:** Guidelines for selection and use.	Provides an overview of the quality concepts and the models which can be used to implement them.
9001	**Quality systems:** Model for quality assurance in design, development, production, installation, and servicing.	Used when conformance to specification requirements during design, development, production, installation, and servicing is required.
9002	**Quality systems:** Model for quality assurance in production and installation.	Used when conformance to specification requirements is limited to production and installation.
9003	**Quality systems:** Model for quality assurance in final inspection and test.	Used when conformance to specification requirements is to be assured by the supplier solely at final inspection and test.
9004	**Quality systems:** Model for quality management and quality systems.	Used for developing and implementing an internal quality system for design and manufacturing.

ISO and CQI

The ISO standards are directed toward improving a firm's production processes. A CQI system can be viewed as the big picture and is concerned with customer satisfaction and all activities conducted by a firm. Although one could correctly argue that leadership is required for a successful ISO program, the leader as described in the CQI model provided by the Baldrige Award structure is far more encompassing. Thus, a good way to view ISO is that the emphasis in the ISO registration process is on the management of process quality.

A CQI System versus an ISO System

This is not meant to minimize the role of ISO in a CQI system. The ISO standards provide an excellent beginning point for a firm starting a CQI system. Obtaining control over the management of process quality is fundamental to the survival of a firm.

ISO Registration

A firm must first decide which of three levels of certification to obtain: ISO 9001, 9002, or 9003. (ISO 9000 is an overview and ISO 9004 is used for internal quality rather than outside certification.) A couple of critical questions can be asked to determine which registration to seek. Firms engaged in design effort and/or after-sale servicing typically seek ISO 9001 registration. ISO 9002 registration is for firms involved in production and installation that produce to other firms' specifications (that is, they do not have a design function). Thus, ISO 9002 registration is less demanding than ISO 9001. ISO 9003 is typically sought by distributors and retailers.

The key to registration is the third-party audit conducted by a registrar. Not only must a firm pass this audit, but most registrars conduct on-site audits twice per year after registration is achieved.

A beginning point for firms seeking an ISO registrar is to ask the key customers in their industry who they recommend. The cost of ISO registration is not excessive, and often the internal evaluation of policies and procedures will result in savings that offset that cost of implementation. Be sure the registrar uses auditors who are familiar with the practices employed in your industry. If your firm is selling in the European market, use a registrar that is recognized and accepted by that nation.

Who Does What in ISO?

Responsibilities in implementing ISO are shown below, beginning with top management's creation of a quality policy. This general policy forms the "thrust" for the firm. It must be posted and known by all employees. Customers should also be aware of this policy.

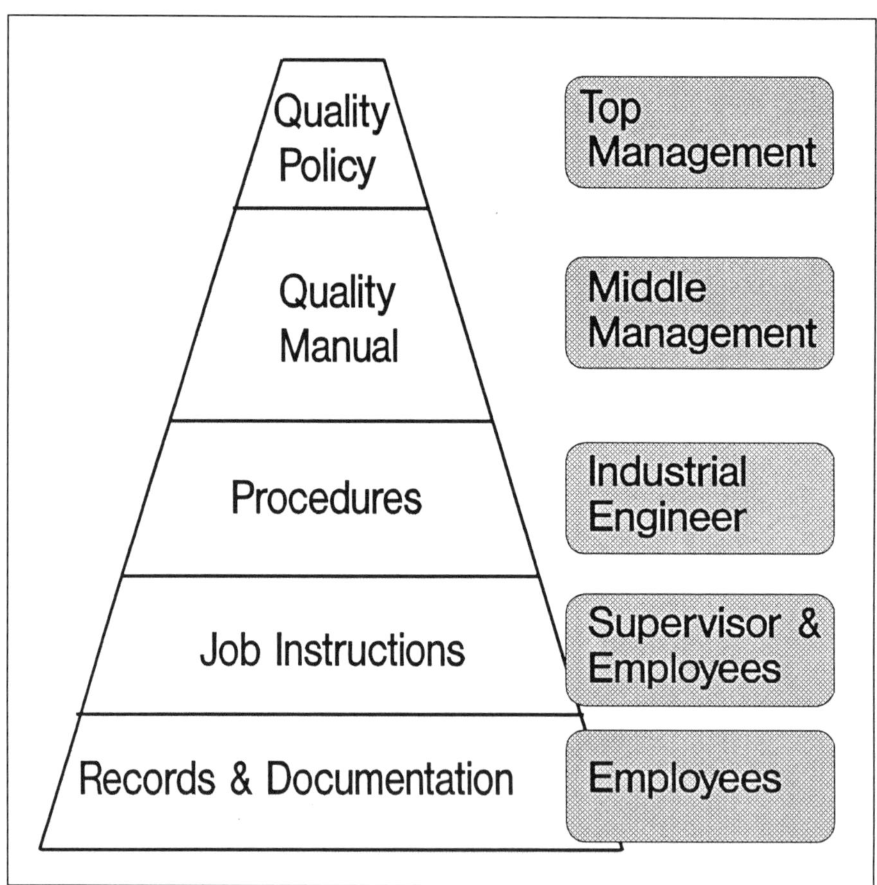

ISO Documentation Responsibilities

The quality manual is usually a statement of the key quality policies and provisions for the firm. To keep the paperwork manageable, procedures are normally referenced but are not included in the manual. However, the procedures must be available on-site so that they can be referred to and followed by employees. Detailed job instructions on critical processes are referenced in the procedures and kept on-site. Adequate records and documentation must be kept to demonstrate that quality products are being produced.

All policies, procedures, and pertinent data must be documented and ready for inspection at any time. It is the responsibility of the employees to follow the instructions laid out by the quality procedures and to keep accurate documentation of their work. A member of the management team is assigned the role of internal auditor to assure that all employees are correctly trained and are following the procedures.

For additional information, see two articles by Pete Mears: "An ISO 9000 Certified Pizza Isn't All that Far-Fetched" (*Journal for Quality and Participation,* October–November 1993, pp. 20–23) and "A Systematic Process for Identifying Goals to Achieve Continuous Quality Improvement" (*Journal for Quality and Participation,* in press).

Endnote

1. Pete Mears, "A Systematic Process for Identifying Goals to Achieve Continuous Quality Improvement," *Journal for Quality and Participation,* in press.

Exercise 35

Do We Need ISO?

Instructions:

Based on what you have read and know about ISO, brainstorm whether or not the management team should investigate ISO further. (It is not necessary to separate into your assigned teams.)